THEOLOGY AND BODY

THEOLOGY AND BODY

Edited by
JOHN Y. FENTON

THE WESTMINSTER PRESS
Philadelphia

Published by The Westminster Press®
Philadelphia, Pennsylvania

PRINTED IN THE UNITED STATES OF AMERICA

Library of Congress Cataloging in Publication Data

Conference on Theology and Body, Emory University,
  1973.
  Theology and body.

  Sponsored by Columbia Theological Seminary, Emory
University, and the Interdenominational Theological
Center.
  Includes bibliographical references.
  1. Man (Theology)—Congresses. I. Fenton, John Y.,
ed. II. Columbia Theological Seminary, Decatur, Ga.
III. Emory University, Atlanta. IV. Interdenominational
Theological Center, Atlanta. V. Title.
BT702.C66 1973   233   74–13404
ISBN 0–664–20712–X

CONTENTS

INTRODUCTION

William A. Beardslee

"Theology and Body" as a phrase has an awkwardness that suggests unfinished business. These essays and the discussion that goes with them are designed to challenge traditional theology and show where it needs to grapple with some things that it has neglected. This is not so much a book that takes theological positions as it is one that opens up questions that theologians need to deal with.

The book arose from a conference on "Theology and Body" held in Atlanta in October 1973. At the conference an effort was made to establish a dialogue among those who stand at the boundary of theological and cultural exploration and those who express themselves in more traditional religious ways. The conference was strikingly interdisciplinary. It succeeded in bringing together some two hundred fifty students, professors, ministers, clinical psychologists, social workers, and physicians in discussion of the issues. One reason for the particular choice of topics was the desire to combine traditional oral presentation with nonverbal bodily awareness. Thus, therapy sessions were a prominent feature of the meetings.

Some treatments of the body in theology move, so to speak, outward from a core of established religious tradition and enrich this tradition with a deeper awareness of our bodiliness. In contrast, this collection of papers moves from the circumference and points toward issues of converging concern about our embodied nature. These are issues about which there is no consensus as yet.

But whatever our theological perspective, we need to confront this range of issues: the mind-body problem (Richard Zaner); the body as shaper of our world (Bernard Aaronson, Richard Zaner, and all the writers); the body as the source of direct feeling, but also of historical limitation (Sam Keen and Tom Driver); the body as what makes social interaction possible and also as one important obstacle to community (Gwen Kennedy Neville, Cecil W. Cone, and John W. Gill). Julia Fenton's *Bodies/An Artwork* dramatized the concreteness of bodily location in a way that charmed many and irked a few.

Thus the book is offered as a challenge to the reader to rethink a whole cluster of theological and religious positions in a way that takes bodily existence more seriously.

The reader can quickly see that most of the authors here will be telling him that Western theology has not taken the body seriously enough, and that among its meanings, "body" suggests directness of feeling and an affirmation of the power of life. Sam Keen and Tom Driver both make these points effectively.

At the same time, the reader should be aware that much the same emphasis on directness of felt experience and on the positive affirmation of life appears in other settings under the term "spirit" rather than "body," for instance in charismatic and Pentecostal movements. From different parts of our religious culture, people groping toward the affirmation of the same realities choose such different words to describe what they are talking about. That is one of the signs of the openness of our theological situation and of the need to take one another seriously.

Part of the problem with "body" arises from the fact that we are not nearly so clear about what a body is, or what it is to be embodied, as we usually suppose. Richard Zaner addresses this question of embodiment in a difficult but rewarding essay, which is designed from a philosopher's point of view to help religious thinkers become aware of what they often take for granted, the problematic reality that we are our bodies, yet transcend them. Tom Driver's presentation of a concrete, bodily experience as a context for reflection makes this same point. Bernard Aaronson attacks the same problem of embodiment as a psychologist, with evidence of how our "mental" perceptions are shaped and limited by our particular body constitution, so that mind and body imply each other. To the subject-object forms of perception he opposes "direct perception," which he associates with the void. Thus he points toward an issue also raised by Sam Keen, who speaks of the void and of how "something happens between the synapses" as an opening to freedom and by Julia Fenton's *Bodies/An Artwork*, with its strong display of randomness. All these in their various ways challenge the traditional association of the mystery of the divine with orderliness, since they all associate orderliness with the world of objectivity, which as such appears lifeless.

The note of affirmation and celebration associated with the body is counterbalanced by Sam Keen's reminder that a bodily or erotic theology does not take one out of the terror and loneliness of existence, but gives a more concrete frame in which to be precariously human. The three sections of Chapter IV by Gwen Kennedy Neville, Cecil W. Cone, and John W. Gill even more sharply present the body as the instrument of concrete social existence with its limitations and its injustices. These sections serve as a strong, even bitter reminder that a turn to bodily theology is not to be an escape from our mutual responsibility for each other.

Every part of the book is rich in materials for religious and theological reflection. The final chapter, by John Y. Fenton, which was not part of the original conference, offers a direct theological confrontation with the meaning of "body." It is marked by its differentiation of the Christian tradition as body-affirming from the more body-negating Eastern traditions, an emphasis noteworthy as coming from one with close personal familiarity with the practice of meditation. It is also distinguished by its affirmation of acceptance of the body and of limitedness in the context of grace.

This book limits itself primarily to oral and written presentations. We have not found it possible to re-create for the printed page the nature and effect of the four "Body Therapy" sessions. These were "Explorations in Embodiment," led by Sam Keen; "Gestalt Awareness in Theological Teaching: Getting Our Bodies Involved," led by Tom Driver; and two groups on "Movement Expression," led by Katie Shearer Schane, teacher of dance at Georgia State University, and Carol Taylor, teacher at the DeKalb School of Ballet. About these sessions John Fenton remarked that they were the "warm" part of the conference, and perhaps this terse comment can qualify them for the purposes of this introduction.

We have included, in an appendix, however, an account of the opening event of the conference, *Bodies/An Artwork*, by Julia Fenton. Intentionally puzzling, like a Zen *koan*, this piece reminds the reader both of the concrete "hereness" of bodily existence and of the immense gap, often obscured in traditional forms of art and writing, between the lived moment and the "deposit" of that moment in a "work."

It need hardly be said that there are other fruitful aspects of the problems arising from a theological focus on the body besides those raised here. One reason for choosing the particular emphases represented here was that they lent themselves to the combination of traditional verbal discourse and nonverbal therapy which the conference was designed to express.

For one of the aims of the conference was to combine discursive thinking and oral interchange with more immediate and nonverbal "bodily" awareness. These chapters still bear the form of their spoken presentation, and intentionally so, to be a reminder of the more-than-intellectual nature of the subject. We hope that the reader will respond to this in-

formality, even though from the point of view of the finished
essay it is a mark of incompleteness. Sam Keen felt this point
so strongly that he specifically wanted to say that "oral communication is inexact and much of it depends on gesture
and the presence of bodies," and that a "transcript carries
neither the force of the living word nor the grace of an essay."
But the countervailing asset of such a group of statements is
their directness and the vivid way in which, especially in discussion, the authors engage each other.

The Conference on Theology and Body was planned by a
committee of which John Y. Fenton was chairman, and his
was the leading spirit throughout. It has fallen to me to write
this brief introduction only because he had to leave for a
sabbatical period just before completing the finishing touches
for the book. The other members of the committee were
Earl C. Brown, Georgia State University; John C. Diamond,
Interdenominational Theological Center; Eduard N. Loring,
Columbia Theological Seminary; William Mallard, Emory
University; and Richard D. Parry, Agnes Scott College; and
myself. The conference was held at Emory University and
was sponsored by Columbia Theological Seminary, Emory
University, and the Interdenominational Theological Center,
with the collaboration of The Westminster Press. To these
and to others as well who contributed to the vitality of the
conference, the committee expresses its warm thanks, as well
as to Ms. Joan Baird and Ms. Arlene Gross for careful work
on the typescript.

I

TOWARD AN EROTIC THEOLOGY *

Sam Keen

It's hard to begin a conference about Theology and Body.
Whenever you talk about theology, you have to decide
whether you're going to talk as a disembodied person, as a
disembodied mind, or as somebody who *is* a body. Theology
has been done largely as an elaboration of the logos and not
too much in terms of the actual body.

It has been a matter of chronos rather than of kairos; of
abstraction rather than of persons; of an official story rather
than of personal stories.

This brings me to the problem. It's very hard for me to
talk right now in an incarnate way. I've just flown from California, where it's now five minutes until five. That's a horrible
hour for energy-type "B" people. Energy-type "B" people are
those who get up fast, and go hard until five o'clock in the
afternoon. Then—*wham!* Suddenly no energy! The best thing
to do if nothing is there is to let nothing be there. Energy-
type "B" people are very fortunate, because their rhythms
coincide with a certain natural-mystical cycle of the universe.
As Irish fairy tales tell us, twilight is a time when you can
very easily slip between the two worlds. So if it happens to
be your time of nothingness, you may be able to slip into
the other world. If I were going to be really honest with

---

* See Sam Keen's remarks on oral communication, quoted on p. 11.

what my body wanted to do now, I'd probably sit and medi-
tate with you and see if we could all slip into the other world.

But I guess I'd better not do that, so I'm going to take the
next best course, which is to act like a theoretical thinker
until I recover enough of my soul to tell stories.

Let me start with some facts and analyses. I think we're
in the middle of a religious situation that is unparalleled to
any since the rise of the Christian era.

Seven or eight years ago we had a conference here, on
America and the Future of Theology. It was in some senses
the death knell of theology. Tom Altizer, Bill Hamilton, Paul
van Buren, and others told us God was dead. They told us
so in a rather conservative way, and for a long time the magazines picked it up. And then something happened—that is,
nothing! Theology went on as if the "death of God" theology
movement had not existed. Academic theology kept going,
yet there seemed to be less and less life in it. Theology as a
discipline didn't know where to go. After the "death of God"
theology, there was no theological method that recommended
itself to those who were not already convinced of the validity
of the theological circle. The "death of God" theology did not
wrestle with the most difficult theological question—the question of finding who owns the Kingdom, the Power, and the
Glory. When Altizer said God had told him that God was
dead, somehow it didn't get to the heart of the real skeptic,
and when van Buren and Hamilton said, "Let's just do away
with God, but keep his only-begotten Son," it didn't get to
the radical problem of theology. And so people who were in
formal theological institutions and churches heaved a sigh
of relief and went on as if a radical challenge had not been
issued to formal theology. Our theological institutions have
gone on, our form of theological thinking has gone on, and
it has gotten more and more pale, and more and more out
of contact with the culture. Meanwhile, back at the ranch,
something else of great significance has been happening to
which the people in the churches don't seem yet to have
caught on. Namely, that we're in the middle of the largest

religious revolution the West has ever seen.

If ten years ago you had predicted that we would have a moral revolution, such as represented by the New Left, or a religious revolution, such as has been represented by the intrusion of the Eastern disciplines—yoga, Hare Krishna, ARICA Institute, and transcendental meditation—people would probably have said: "You're nuts! It can't possibly happen. East is East, and West is West, and certainly the pragmatic American psyche isn't going to buy that kind of thing." Yet here it is. It's happening. We are creating a whole new category of people who are trying different life-styles, new religious disciplines. The books on Zen, Yoga, and Eastern religion that are in every drugstore are a pretty accurate index of what's going on. So, here we have a situation in which Western religion, the Judeo-Christian tradition, is losing its vitality. At the same time, we have an intrusion of a new religious spirit.

The new revolution is contrary to most of the things the Christian tradition has stood for.

First of all, it is mystical. It's anti-professional. It's bodily, it's erotic, it's cosmic. It does not deal too much with the transcendental God. Those of us who have any interest in the Christian tradition and the preservation either of Christian theology, or Christian anthropology, or of Christian spirituality have to ask ourselves very quickly, "What is worth preserving within the Christian tradition?" We have to ask this question in a far more radical way than the demythologization movement of Bultmann or radical theology asks it. We have to go down to the level of anthropology to ask the question: "What is it in the Christian view of man, and the world, that is worthy of preservation and how can we preserve it?"

Just to state my own convictions, I am rather suspicious of the intrusions of Eastern disciplines into the West. You can interpret the new emphasis on meditation and fantasy as evidence that we're finally maturing; we're finally slowing down. But danger is involved when meditation becomes more central than action. Those who are most interested in meditation are also least interested in conflict. In places such as the ARICA

Institute the effort is to do away with conflict, to interpret all conflict as problems within the ego. The ego is to be reduced so people can live at peace. One of the parts of the Christian tradition that I've always liked is that it's for warfare. The prophets weren't nice people; you wouldn't have wanted them in your house. They were aware that there is a price that is too great to pay for peace, that the world in which we live, the world that God has chosen to create and incarnate himself within, is an agonal world. It's a world in which there is conflict. It's a world in which there is battle. It is in the struggle between good and evil that man is given the arena in which he is supposed to work out his own humanity.

The Eastern position is very much against that. With Eastern spirituality went a stratification of society in which spirituality was squeezed upward so that a class society was created with the elite, the Brahmans, and those who were into meditation and the cosmic consciousness on top; and at the bottom were the untouchables.

A very lively and almost completely unasked question is: "To what degree does the cultivation of cosmic consciousness destroy the impulse toward social justice? To what degree does it destroy the toleration of conflict which must be an element in the building of any more equitable society?" That at least must be asked in the present situation.

Theology is dead. But there are a lot of live theologians left. And religion is very much alive. Maybe theology and religion can get together again in our time. Maybe we're standing at a unique crossroads in human history where, for the first time, East and West may be able to meet. Maybe we can salvage what the Christian tradition had to say about man, about justice, about grace, and still not have to pay the terrible price of accepting repressive attitudes about the body and sexuality.

Let me talk more about that. Now I'm beginning confession time. Confession is good for the soul. I think theology conferences are like prayer meetings anyway. We usually disguise the language. I'm angry at Christians for not being Christians. I read in my church history that the first struggle that Christianity had was with Gnosticism. Against all the Greek dualistic impulses, the early church theologians insisted that the message of Christianity was that somehow God came into the flesh, that he sanctified history, that he incarnated himself in the here and now. What I observe actually and functionally is that Christianity and Christian theology have functioned largely in the same way as Gnosticism. The essence of Gnosticism was dualism. Dualism! Let me list some of the dualisms that we have retained. Christianity and Judaism begin with a fundamental dualism from which I think all other dualisms follow: the dualism between man and God. In the beginning is God and then man. All of you can run the table now if you remember your Barthian theology: God and man, grace and nature, church and world, revelation and reason. A good psychotherapist would look at these dualisms and see paranoia. He would say: "Ha, ha. That means the world is divided into us and them."

These dualisms are one source of the alienation of our times because they are congruent with other dualisms: spirit and matter, mind and body, capital and labor, mind workers and body workers, upper classes and lower classes. These hierarchies are built into us. We all know that rich people are better than poor people; that mind workers are better than people who work with their bodies; that whites are better than blacks; that men are better than women. We know it. That's why we have to deny it, because those hierarchies are so deeply inbred into us. Incidentally, these dualisms were perpetuated by Freud, who was supposed to be our great liberator but who in fact put Ego, and Super Ego, against the Libido. Christianity and capitalism have combined to alienate us from the natural world and from the body. Christianity killed the great god Pan, and it provided the metaphysics that allowed us to desecrate the earth, because it was no longer sacred. The earth was merely the mass on which God worked.

Christian theology and practice separated us from the world, from nature, and from our own sexuality, because sexuality is the point where nature makes its voice heard within us. Therefore, in this kind of dualistic scheme, anytime that matter or nature starts to upsurge, the best thing to do is to contain it quickly; you know, get the logos around it in a hurry! Teach Johnny to read by the time he's two years old or he might have an experience he can't conceptualize; or worse, a feeling; or even worse than that, a sensation! And if the devil's after him that day, he might even have a sexual sensation. All these pure kids having sexual sensations. Incredible idea! Freud was almost lynched for the very idea, and that reaction is still deep in our culture. We have been cut off at some fundamental level from our own bodies. Even our language reflects it. We talk about having bodies as if there were a difference between the possessor and the possessed.

And now, I want to shift the story. I used to love that old hymn, ". . . Tell me the old, old stories I love to hear." You know retelling the story is the glory. I told the story of the repressive nature of theology one way, and if you don't like it that way, I'll tell it another way. I'll tell the same story but tell it autobiographically.

This is the story of that same split, but the story of how that split happened to me, and what kinds of things I've been doing in order to try to find a way through the split for myself.

First of all, no Christian theology I ever read (exception: Aarne Siirala, *The Voice of Illness;* Fortress Press, 1964) dealt with the fact that there is a physiology of alienation. There is a physiology of estrangement. If you're going to talk about sin and about estrangement, and if you really believe that man is a psychosomatic unity, then you'd better talk about muscle structure. You'd better talk about enzymes, you'd better talk about *what actually happens in the body* when a man is cut off from himself, when he's estranged from himself and estranged from other things. The most fundamental

fact of human existence is that we all are bodies. But theology
has dealt so little with the physiology of alienation and the
physiology of grace. Can we talk about grace and disgrace?
Is grace not a bodily concept? Is disgrace not a bodily concept? Can't we specify what it means to be a graceful and
a disgraceful body? Well, I was raised in the Christian tradition and I think my story really is every Christian's story to
some degree or the other, and that's why I want to tell it.

I was WASP—White Anglo-Saxon Protestant. And worse
than that, a Southern Presbyterian. If you've read anything
of the sexual surveys or anything like that, you know we're
hard core. You know Masters and Johnson have clinics where
they treat impotence and frigidity, and they have ninety-nine
successes and one failure which is inevitably a White Anglo-
Saxon Protestant Southern fundamentalist. We don't rate so
high on the frequency either, if you notice. As a matter of
fact, when we did the sex survey in *Psychology Today,* we
tried to get predictive factors. The only predictive factor we
could come up with that held about the quality of a person's
sexual experience was his religious background. The more
religious, the less sexy.

So, I was a WASP and you know WASP's have large
thoraxes and small waists; again that is the American ideal.
That is the body type that incarnates American virtues of
seriousness and self-containment. I suppose there were three
things that you could've gotten kicked out for in the Presbyterian Church: doctrinal heresy, laughing, and having an
erection or its equivalent in church. None of those were per-
missible in the church at all unless you were Elmer Gantry.
Baptists were not as high on the scale, because we all knew
they were lower down in the Mass, less intellectual. We had
the logos more firmly incarnate in our doctrines. We knew
how things were. The Baptists were sort of emotional; they
weren't as bad as the Holy Rollers and people like that, but
they were emotional, and that's bad. I really dug all that
stuff, for some reason. I saved war stamps and put them in

my book. I saved $40 in quarters and bought books on birds, and binoculars, and looked at the birds and knew the Latin names before I was twelve, and was lecturing the Women's Society of Maryville, Tennessee, on the Latin names of birds —which must have fascinated them. If you memorized all that Latin and you're twelve, what are you going to do except show somebody that you know it?

One of my earliest memories is of lying on the sleeping porch in Sebring, Florida. I must have been four, and it was nap time (which was abomination, because they didn't tell you in those days you took a nap because your mother was tired. We were not hyperkinetic in those days, because we didn't have a concept of hyperkinetic kids. We just had kids). Anyway, I was lying there and what else can you do if you're four years old and you have to lie there for an hour and a half? So I started playing with myself. It seemed like a reasonable thing to do. My mother stuck her head through the window and said, "Nice boys don't do that." Well, that kind of message was perfectly appropriate for Southern Presbyterians who did believe that God created the world, that he created man—from the waist up, or at least, from the neck up. There was some allowance for emotions as long as they were channeled in orderly ways. But certainly from the waist down it was understood that any kind of emotions or sensations connected with that area were appropriate only after duly ordained matrimony, preferably experienced at night, and in one position at most. Well, at about fifteen, I began to notice that there was something the matter with my body. (It wasn't what you think—it's worse than that!) I lost a fight and you don't lose fights, because competitiveness and productivity are good virtues. So if you lose a fight, it shows that you're something less than a man—a sissy, at the very least. So I did "the thing." I took a Charles Atlas course. I swear that I actually did. It was a clandestine affair from the start, because we weren't allowed to read comic books. So first I had to get the comic book in order to get the coupon to send away for the Charles Atlas course. Well, I did it, and when the instructions arrived I would go upstairs every day and do dynamic tension. Before long I was very proud of my new arm muscles. Then I saw Greek statues that showed the pectoral muscles—they were the great ones. At first every boy falls in love with biceps. "I was a skinny kid, but you'll kick sand in *my* face no more!" The biceps are the clues to everything. But then you get more sophisticated, because you find that the biceps are connected to the triceps. And then there's the arms, and the chest, and next you fall in love with these. Everybody knows you strengthen the chest muscles with barbells; dynamic tension helps, but barbells are best, and push-ups. Once I had my chest muscles developed, I began to worry about my stomach. My stomach did not look like the Marlboro man. I had the picture before my eyes of how I was supposed to look—like a slim version of a gorilla. Well, I did it! And I did it so well I convinced myself that if I didn't exercise and work out every day, I would disintegrate in two days. I had two days' grace before disintegration. I made an American body. A Christian body and an American body are very much the same. The body I constructed was typically American, because it was constructed in terms of an image of what a body should be. The image of the American body is a body that is constructed to work, not to play. It's constructed for the dominance of the head. It's a capitalistic body—a body ruled by the head.

All you have to do to verify this hypothesis is to join me now for a minute and assume the ideal American posture. Sit up straight. You know the archetype of this is the West Point posture. So if you would, scoot out to the edge of your seat and, for once in your life, do exactly what mother was constantly telling you to do: Get your shoulders back, get your back straight, pull in your stomach as much as you can, throw your chest out and your shoulders back; and keeping that stomach in, breathe! Now, if any of you here can feel your genitals in this position without using your hands, you get a free Charles Atlas course. Why do we construct bodies like that? There is a logic to the ideal types that society projects. The American body ideal is projected in such a way that you're sucking the guts up into the diaphragm and you're inflating the chest—the ego area. This is also the physiology of emphysema, where you inflate the chest and deflate the stomach. Also, it forces the ego upward. More and more, the directing center of the human personality is in the head. Just to see the contrast, look at a statue of a Buddha. The Buddha is letting it all hang out! That's the essence of Eastern disciplines, where their bodies are different. If you think of the body as having four centers (the head center; the heart center; the kath center, or hara; and the genitals), in American theology we have a descending order of valuation. The head has the most dignity, the genitals the least. To be in control is most important, to conceptualize, to be able to use words. Next in importance is to have some kind of care. But preferably have that care romantic and preferably keep it well in control of the head. Then as we get down into instincts (instincts are what makes birds migrate and animals rut, and that's not a very human thing to do), it's best to keep them under control. When we get to the genitals we don't talk about them. It's all right to do *it* (sex) occasionally, but you don't *talk* about it in theology. So you see the descending order of importance. In Eastern thought, it's exactly the opposite. The center of the personality is said to be in the hara—four inches below the navel. The key is to get rid of the chatter in the head. This is the same thing Carlos Castaneda means when he says, "Learn to stop the world." In Zen thought, the head must be blank. In Nirvana, there is no head. That doesn't mean that nothing is going on in the head; it means that the moving principle is in the center. When you transfer the center of the personality to the hara, you locate the center of the personality in the guts rather than in the head. A good wrestler keeps his eyes on his opponent's stomach because whenever he moves, he has to move from there. That is the center from which you move. You watch there and you can't be faked out.

Now what this implies is that in Eastern thought there is an entirely different anthropology, and it is not an anthropology of triumph. It does not say that the head can triumphantly rule the body. It says that the human personality and its incarnation in the world has to begin from the movement center. And once you're into motion as a dominant factor, you're into emotion. How can one feel without moving? There are very few things you can feel without moving. That's why Nietzsche said to one of his enemies who confessed that he could write only when sitting down: "Aha, now I have you, you nihilist. The only thoughts that are worthwhile are those that are arrived at while walking." And Aristotle—bless his heart—was called a peripatetic, which doesn't mean he was on the road all the time, but he did walk in order to think. The ideal Eastern body is so different from the American body. The American body is constructed by the mirror to conform to an appearance of slimness.

We call it style. Did you ever think what a demonic notion style is—style of dress? It says that my relationship to you is going to be determined by how I present myself—the image that I present to you. Not by touch. Sight is safer, so that's why we use it. Let's just say it's head-oriented, capitalistic.

At any rate, I realized that I had an American body. I was caught between the sexual commands of St. Paul (Don't!) and those of the Marlboro man (Do!). I was caught between the toughness taboo and the tenderness taboo in the body I had made for myself. Being an orthodox Presbyterian, I did have a head full of the right ideas. I did what God did. Namely, God transcended the world, God remained at a great distance from the world and interceded through his Son and occasionally his Spirit. But, essentially, he was up there. By the criterion that said Christians were supposed to emulate the image of God, I did pretty well. I was paranoid. I existed at a great distance from other people. I remained largely in my head. After having cultivated all these Christian virtues, I couldn't understand why I was angry all the time; why, although I had all this belief, I didn't trust anybody, most of all myself. How was I to get out of prison? But this ends part one of the story. Now I'm going on to the development of Erotic Theology.

I had the good fortune when I had a sabbatical to have a choice between going to Tübingen and studying German (I didn't learn German in my doctoral work very well, and I thought that if I was ever going to be a real scholar, I'd better learn German—it's the original theological language) or going to California. So I made the decision on what I thought were reasonable grounds. I always wanted to learn to surf, and that's hard to do in Tübingen. So I went to California and I got involved in encounter groups. I went crazy, and I got Rolfed and I did a lot of other things, including finally a breakup of my marriage. I turned my back on theology and left all institutions and became a free-lancer.

For a long time I thought I could get myself totally free from theology, that the only way to re-own the body was to realize that theology was essentially a repressive discipline; that what Tom Altizer said here seven years ago was right— "God is the transcendent ground of repression." Now I'm finding out that I can't leave theology, or that, worse yet, it won't leave me. My being is somehow centered in something theology once used to talk about—the concept of the sacred. My understanding of my body, my experience of my body, is centered in something that is sacred and erotic. That's what I want to talk about now. What would an erotic theology look like if we got rid of the dualisms I spoke about earlier? Could we talk about something sacred, something holy, in a way that would allow us to stop being strangers to ourselves? Could we stop suffering from the kinds of alienation that Christian metaphysics and capitalist society have imposed on us?

Let me start with a model. I believe that the old theology produced neurotic individuals. The split in man was accentuated by the dualisms of Christianity and of capitalism. An erotic theology is going to have to produce a new type of *person*. Notice I didn't say a new type of man. The new person will be as deeply feminine as masculine. The whole concept is going to be elaborated, not from a male position at all, but from a male and a female position. The new person is going to be a "cosmopolitan lover." You probably all know I'm cheating already, because I'm smuggling in three ideas: *cosmos, polis,* and *eros.* The new person is going to be characterized as one who is organized around those three kinds of realities.

Let me talk about *cosmos* first. The earth itself is sacred. It's quite clear that there is no solution to the ecological crisis without a return to the notion of the sacred character of the earth. The sacred is to be interpreted as being homogenized *into* the world rather than transcending the world. *This* is a sacred place. *This is* holy ground. Nobody lives in Palestine anymore. The whole theological notion that we have to filter our awareness of the Holy through one given point in human history (Jesus Christ) is, as near as I can determine it, the *cause* of our alienation and not the solution of our alienation. God has come outdoors, he's everywhere. He's not the captive of the clergy. He's not the captive of institutions. He's not the captive even of religious concepts or language about God. An erotic theology repaganizes the world in a very substantial way. The pagan view of things, the tragic view of things, considered the whole world as sacred. It was the movement of the cosmos that was the index of its divinity.

Second is the idea of *polis.* We are not merely individuals. We start as individuals in some way; or at least to know ourselves we have to know our individual stories. But we are also essentially political beings. If we do not start with *we,* we never get to we. The essence of the old theology, as I understand it, is that it started with a paranoid assumption about

the world, and projected that paranoia onto God. It started
with the idea of *us* and *them*. The brotherhood of man was always talked about, but the brothers who were not of The Faith
were not of equal value with the brothers of The Faith. Functionally, within Christian institutions, theologians worked to
exclude those who were different from themselves. I think any
kind of erotic theology has to begin with the fact of love, not
with the fact of alienation. In Western philosophy and Western theology you begin by positing man's alienation from
himself and his world. Descartes's *cogito ergo sum* means here
I am, and there is the world, out there. For three hundred
years philosophers wondered, "How do I get to the world?"
But if I am not already in the world, I can never get there.
Even Martin Buber missed the point, because at some levels
there is no "I and Thou." We are already united. Why haven't
we been able to deal with ESP, clairvoyance, and phenomena
of that kind? For hundreds of years we have known of vali-
datable experiences of ESP and clairvoyance, yet no scientist
ever tested them. Why? For obvious reasons. They didn't
have a theory of mind that would allow them to admit that
such phenomena existed. If we aren't separate, if we begin
in some kind of pool, if consciousness is a unity, if in the beginning is not the word, but the unity, it becomes much
easier to explain these phenomena, even psychokinesis. The
only way that I can begin to allow paranormal psychological
data to present themselves to my mind is by understanding
in some way that the universe is a universe. The ties that bind
it together are, somehow, spiritual ties. We are in communion
—*we are*.

The third thing is that Erotic Theology begins with *eros*.
The kind of love that ruled the hierarchy in the old scheme of
things was *agape*, unselfish love. I think an erotic theology
has got to begin with eros, which is to say we have to begin
with desire. Desire. Huston Smith somewhere says that Hinduism says, "If you want something, go after it." It was also
Augustine's insight, "Love and do what you want." But we

never followed it in Western Christianity. Desire is the way to the Holy. Do what you want. Follow your desire, not your duty. Your desire will take you to the path of God. Somehow that's the same thing as saying that the essence of man is essentially trustworthy. But what this means is that we have to develop an entirely new way of looking at and thinking about sexuality. We have to throw out the notion of sexual morality as being a codeable phenomenon. The question is: "Who is involved? In what way?" Autobiography determines the nature of sexuality.

Why is this theology? Where is something Holy seen in this? I know these are questions which people who are formally interested in theology have. How do you know? Where do we look within our bodies, within our experience, to find the revelation of the Holy? I think we have to go back to Rudolf Otto's basic notion of what it means to say that something is Holy. What are the earmarks of that which is Holy or sacred? Otto says that wherever you find yourself in the presence of the Holy, there are three phenomena: First of all, a *mysterium*. You are in the presence of something mysterious that is something Wholly Other. That mystery has two defining characteristics. It is *tremendum* and *fascinans*. It is tremendous and awe-inspiring. Before it you tremble, and it is desirable. It draws you to it. So I think that gives us the criteria for finding the holy.

In the first place, the mystery. To say that the mystery of God is in our bodies is to say that God is no place; that is, no place specific. When you get to the Holy of Holies, it is always empty. The void is our teacher. I think these four words are functionally the same: God, Grace, Freedom, Nothingness. They all refer to the same basic phenomena: at the heart of what we know as holy, there is an experience of the bottom dropping out. Suddenly cause and effect doesn't work. Something happens between the synapses. There is a moment when something snaps. After years of moving from compulsion to compulsion, from tightness to tightness, the obsessive compulsion or estrangement breaks. Where there was a whole, a complete system of organized compulsions, suddenly there's a hole, a space, a silence. Where before there was cause-effect, cause-effect, cause-effect, and you experience your own captivity, suddenly there's a nothingness, a void. And when you come out of the void, something new is born. So the mystery in us is always related to the fact of our being empty in some significant sense. There is no mystery of God without the experience of human emptiness. You can't be filled if you're not hungry. The hunger of the human spirit is a perpetual part of human condition. We are not meant to be without hunger. We are not meant to be without nothingness. We are not meant to be without depression. We are not meant to be without panic. We are not meant to be without any of those empty, hungry, spaces that cluster in the chest. Because, if there were no places like that, if there were no points of boredom, there would be nothing that could begin again. And grace is beginning again.

The second is the idea of *tremendum.* You can usually identify the presence of the Holy or the demonic, because in the presence of the Holy or the demonic, you tremble. Ask yourself where have you trembled in the last years, and you have a good index of what you know about the Holy.

And the third is the idea of desire (*fascinans*). Pleasure is a great teacher. I think an erotic theology would say there are four great human teachers that will be with you all of your life: pleasure and pain, love and loneliness. This is the essence of an erotic theology. These are the points where we find grace.

But that also defines a certain kind of problem. How do we learn to love instability? How do we learn to love our own emptiness? How can we learn to love our madness? Everything in our culture has told us to contain madness, to suspect it. It has told us to fill every conceivable thing; to fill silence with words, to fill space with houses. It's a problem. An erotic theology must also address itself to silence, to emptiness, to madness.

I want to close with a myth that may be the basis of an erotic theology: Once upon a time God was sitting by himself. And he was doing what Aristotle's God did, which was a form of mental masturbation—playing with himself, thinking on himself, projecting his logos. "In the beginning was the word." He was a wordy creature. And all he did all day long was play with possibilities—fantasize and say, "Oh, wouldn't it be nice if . . ." He'd say, "No, maybe I will do that." But he never did anything. And so, one day after he'd been doing this for several eternities, something strange happened. He noticed he was bored. The nothingness around him began to have a stale odor and he said: "Well, this is bad. I don't know how this happened. I have to do something to get out of this." And he said, "Well, maybe I should take a risk, because I've never done anything except play with the word." And so he said: "I think maybe I'll incarnate myself. I think I'll make a world, and make people; I think I'll actualize some possibilities and not others." So he made a world. And then he made human beings very much like himself, with lots of possibilities, and the ability to actualize only a few of them. Then he realized that he didn't know how to solve his own problem, and so he passed it on to us.

The Problem: How do you incarnate the word? How do you integrate the mind and the body? How do you become one? For the Jews, today is the Day of Atonement. What is our day of atonement? To be human is somehow, I think, to enter fully into our own flesh and to share the agony of human history, the agony of God. And I think the vision of a world in the making, and of ourselves in the making, is maybe a vision that is enough to make us all tremble. Maybe that's an erotic place to begin.

Discussion with Sam Keen

Q: If, as you suggest, Christianity is in or approaching the state of collapse right now, can you account for its apparent domination and success over all these years?

A: The combination of Christianity and capitalism has a fantastic survival value because in those stages of history it was necessary to harness our energies in those ways. The kinds of repressions that we visited upon ourselves were necessary in order to create the kind of culture that we have. But I think Marcuse is right. We have created a culture that is now successful enough to give up many of its repressions. Whereas once it was only the repression of those energies that allowed us to fight the tigers, to drain the swamps, to create the machines, to create the culture, now it is only the release of those energies that is going to allow us to survive as a civilization. Because with the bottling of those energies has come also the incredible neurosis of modern man, his disease, his warlike way of dealing with himself and the whole world. Our neurosis succeeded ever so much better than we thought it would and now we can afford to be without it. I think that we can afford, therefore, to pick up elements in the Christian tradition that were always there theologically but were never really operative. Christianity did have a doctrine of nature, did have a doctrine of creation of the world, did have a doctrine of nat-

ural grace. It's just that those things were never operative
institutionally speaking, or were very minimally operative.
Christianity did preach somewhere of the goodness of the
sexual impulse, but that was never the way it came across.

Q: I'd like to hear what you have to say on the subject
of the nature of sexuality in a really bisexual universe
rather than in terms of the God/Man dichotomy or the
man/woman dichotomy.

A: I think wholeness and health in any human being involves
at least psychological bisexuality, but perhaps not actual bisexuality in terms of sexual expression. Jung is the one who
has shown this best. When men reach the crisis of the forties—
especially in this culture—they become possessed by the
anima, by the feminine, the tender side of their personality;
they usually do something crazy, like falling in love with a
young girl and get divorced, and do things like that, and
thereby they find the feminine side of their own personality.
A great deal of the women's movement now is about finding
and owning the masculine side of the woman's personality.
Essentially the kinds of virtues that we have projected onto
the sexes, and for which there is some biological basis, are
human virtues that we need. Each one of us has to actualize
his "masculine" and "feminine" virtues within his own personality. *Seven Arrows* (by Hyemeyohsts Storm; Harper & Row,
1972), a book about the mythology of the American Indian,
talks about the medicine wheel, in which the task of the human being is to go all the way around the medicine wheel. If
you're born in the north, which is cold and you're cold and
wise; or in the east, where everything is clear but you're distant—then your task has got to be to go down into the south,
where things are warm and close, and then go to the west,
where you have intuition. That is the human path of actualiz-
ing the psychological bisexuality. This is, in some sense, in-
troducing the feminine element back into theology, because
the pagan religions were maternal. They focused on the earth,

which was mother, which was sacred, and not upon that which was distant. They didn't focus on the logos. Logos is a male concept.

Q: You said that theology of the body has to be concerned with eros, with cosmos, and with polis. Then I heard you refer to Otto's analysis of the sense of the numinous, but I really didn't see a connection between these two things. I didn't see what's essentially sacred or holy about the body. Why do you have to make that connection?

A: Whenever I ask people: "Where do you tremble?"; "Where have you felt awe?"; "Where have you felt desire more than that which was elicited by a specific situation?"; "Where have you trembled in the last year?"; "Describe what holy means"—almost always the answers, the kinds of experiences they will give, are like this: "Well, I was on a mountaintop"; or, "I was by the ocean." First, the experiences of nature are still sacred to modern man. Second, when we had twenty thousand people in Louisville, Kentucky, with Martin Luther King and we sang and we marched up on the Capitol and we sang "We shall overcome"; or when you and I stood in picket lines when there were fourteen of us and some people said, "Where is Vietnam?"—we trembled, especially when the Marines came down the street in Louisville. So, in community, you ask: "What is the crying search of this age?"; "Who are my people?"; "Where is my community?"

And third, sexuality is a place of trembling, both of the fear and of the promise. Sexuality is still a place where the holy resides. Those are the places where the holy is most manifest in people's experience.

Q: According to Otto, the Holy is *fascinans* and *tremendum* at the same time. It presents itself as both aspects simultaneously. Do you think that this analogy fits the examples of sex and politics and communion?

A: I do, exactly, because the fascination of a northeaster storm is the fascination of the power of nature. All the liveliest sexuality, I think, is always a mixture of fear and desire. As a matter of fact, it's usually a question of who is going to win. I see the demonic pull of these communities, of the communes that are bringing people together. Yet there is the fear of losing themselves. I see them lose themselves in things like ARICA and the Hare Krishna movement; they bring people in, and soon, in order to find themselves, they've shaved their heads and given up their individuality.

Q: What are you going to do with the word? Do you have to take it out?

A: You don't leave the word out. You incarnate the word. I think that we tremble much more before the story than we do before the sermon. Ask yourself, "When have I cried?" Before what words have you cried or had the sense of trembling in the last year? For me, it's been stories. When suddenly somebody's story evoked my own story, and I could say, "Yes, I understand that death." That is where it's at for me. I'm capable of crying in movies when somebody's story is suddenly my story. I'm moved.

A real way to locate the sacred is to locate sacrilege. Every time Nixon comes on, I see so clearly what the sacred is because of its absence. It locates the sacredness of words. Words are sacred when they tell, when they try to reveal, when they're revelatory. And those are the words that move me.

Q: I was wondering why you have theology at all; theology is just words. A new theology would set a new we/they dichotomy.

A: I don't believe in the separation of words and experiences. We have no experience separate from words, because we're linguistic animals. So, if you want to purify experience, you have to purify language; if you want to purify language, you have to purify experience. It's always a dialectic. We can't stop talking, mainly because we need to get to silence. We need to get to the place where words give out. We do theology in order to be done with it.

Q: Sublime experiences on LSD don't need any belief system, any reliance on theology.

A: But it doesn't work. The experiences on acid, more than almost anything else, are determined by the set and the setting. By the expectations you've placed on the drug, what you bring there. The philosophy that goes into an acid trip determines the character of the experience.

Q: This conference is set up for your brains and my brains. I'm hearing the words, but the experience of the body does not come clear.

A: That's right. Nor is it the fault of the setup, I have to say. Aristotle and Raquel Welch reached profound agreement on something. The mind is an erogenous zone. The play of ideas has a sensual content. I suggest that if you tune into your body when words are going on, you will be aware of all kinds of sensations. I'd like to know how my words feel differently in your head than other words. Is this a head trip? It's not a head trip for me. This is my life trip. It doesn't come out of my head at all. It comes out of my own *agon*. It's out of proportion in that you all have not the chance to speak as much as I do. But I have nothing against speaking or ideas, for I believe in them profoundly; I believe there are erotic ideas and there are neurotic ideas. Part of the essence of them is the degree to which you play with different ideas. It has been a strange experience to me to find out that there are feelings in the head. The head actually has sensations within it that are just as vivid as the sensations in any other part of the body. Ideas have a sensory ambience. See how your head feels the next time you are thinking about different things. See when it feels good inside your head. Or, the next time, just after you have been making love, lie there and see what your head feels like. Put all your awareness on the inside of your head, not to what you're thinking. Get in touch with the relationship between what you're thinking and what you're feeling inside the head.

Q: You said, earlier, that the being of your body is something sacred. I've got a feeling that this is maybe an experience you have felt. Have you any way of verbalizing this experience?

A: I'll read you a page from a novel that I'm writing. This is about a character by the name of McNab: "McNab is heard whistling 'I've got plenty of nothing; nothing's plenty for me.' Dionysius the Areopagite would have understood him. The Holy of Holies is always empty. The day of atonement. These realities are in the same place—God, Freedom, The Word, The Place between the Synapses, Silence. Nothing is holy. Everything is. Turn the glove inside out and it fits perfectly. Fantasy and reality switch. All is running something or someone. It's the void that's holy. Everything can begin again there. Drop your anxieties into the void, or let God have them—it's all the same. Keep running after something until you find nothing. You can never find what's looking for you. Be still, and know. Those who run fastest get nowhere first. The prize is defeat. God created the world *ex nihilo*. McNab created himself out of the same stuff." This is as near to an answer to that question as I can come. The answer is *Nothing*.

Q: I want to ask you about eros and, you know, your experience when you were growing up. I associate eros with Plato and that great striving after an ideal. There must be a difference in the eros when you were taking the Charles Atlas course and the eros when you find that kind of beautiful nothing. But then you get scared that it's possible that there isn't any difference. I get the sense of

agape when the Samaritan came down the road and found
this guy. The old version says, "the bowels of compassion."
It was something really at that level; we call that the
center of the body. The Samaritan didn't want to stop
and help that guy. He wasn't sentimental. He wasn't
erotic. He wasn't idealistic. It was something he couldn't
help. It was sort of a bowel-level reaction—"My God, I
can't leave this bastard here!" *Agape* is something you are
quite earthy about. *Eros* bothers me because of that striving, that ideal-grasping. Whether it's when I was Charles
Atlas or whether it's the nothing, how do you know the
difference between one eros and another?

A: It's really a hard question. The clue that I have to this
question is that the eros that leads me astray is largely the
eros of the eyes. When I think I want something, I found out
that what I'm doing is imagining somebody else's eyes looking at me, and seeing those eyes pleased. Let's take clothing
as an example of style. You imagine that you want that shirt
or that thing. That eros is not related to any particular feeling
in your body; it's related to your projection of your own eyes
with the need for approval by somebody else. You see them
seeing you, and when you see their eyes seeing you and ap-
proving of you, then you can finally say, "I'm okay." The
essence of paranoia (the same thing as the Biblical concept
of untrust) is that I observe others watching me and that my
validation in life is always dependent upon their eyes. In
dreams of shame we are usually naked and somebody is watching us. There's a spotlight turned on us. I experience another
kind of eros, another kind of desire, that is much more rooted
at other parts of my body. Yes, the compassion—the bowels
of compassion. When I see somebody injured, I want to vomit.
Of course, that vomiting is also a way of saying: "Don't do
that to flesh. That flesh should not be injured; people should
not be beaten; I am in touch with my own flesh." The revulsion of seeing that is attempting to get in touch with a feeling
in my body, for the eros of the heart.

It's a very, very tricky thing in this society, because we're sold the idea that love is falling in love. "Falling in love" has nothing to do with love, it has to do with loving the other side of yourself. But falling in love is a possession. You could pray to God that it not happen to you, if you can avoid it; because, although the heart thinks it wants something and it projects onto the other person everything that it thinks it desires, it turns out that what it really desired was myself in the other person. Then as you go down, you ask yourself: "What eros is trustable? Is it purely sexual eros?" We at least have the myth that there's an eros that is truly genital. I'm not sure that's true, because, for instance, we define sexually desirable objects in the society in terms of criteria of beauty. The real "lib movement" is not men's lib or women's lib, it's ugly lib. It's liberation from the demonic idea of beauty as having to do with the placement of three inches of flesh. There, again, it's the eyes that are in charge of the eros. So, where is it? I trust my nose a lot. My nose tells me an awful lot. My nose doesn't often lie to me about what it wants. My touch doesn't lie too much. If I get all these things working together, and I get a little vote going, I more or less poll the body politic: Well, you know, she's a good-looking woman, and then my eyes say, "Yeah, yeah, yeah, yeah, yeah," and they maybe transmit a few messages down to the genitals, "Yes, I ratify that." And the heart says, "I don't feel anything," and the mind says, "You know, she doesn't excite me when she talks. I don't want to talk with her." Well, when I get a majority vote, that's the nearest I can come to trusting my body. Like the democratic process, it's wrong as much or more than it's right.

II

THE EXPERIENCE OF THE BODY
AND TRANSCENDENCE

Bernard Aaronson

Much of religious belief is based on the separation of mind and body. Most of us don't like to die, or don't like the idea of death—they aren't the same—and carry ourselves past the point at which we end by conceptions of immortality of the soul or reincarnation. The kind of survival represented by leaving descendants doesn't seem to be enough, nor does the survival represented by leaving books or works of art, or pigeon-bespattered statues in public parks. We want to live.

Indeed, it really is hard to conceive the existence of a time when we didn't live. I know the American Revolution took place, I even have a stamp that I got at the post office the other day that told me that. I know that Marconi invented the telegraph. I know that Jesus walked in Galilee and that Buddha died from eating an ill-advised mushroom stew. I have read these things, or been told about them. They are very interesting stories. They don't have the existential reality of a cavity in my tooth or the fact that I'm standing here and talking to you. Indeed, if the world had been created just five minutes ago, the entire set of events that we know as history, and even the special sets of events that we call our personal histories, would have had to have been set forth in that creation to produce the world which exists right now.

Whatever existed at the time at which we were born or in

our infancies is part of the eternal verity of the universe. I know that radio has existed for only a comparatively short time, and that there are cultures that exist that have no radios. But even though radio has been displaced by television, it is one of the givens of my world. It was there before I was. Similarly, for my son, television and radio are both givens. For me, television is a new technology. For him, it is as much a part of his environment as I am.

Each of us is a center for processing information and for producing additional behavior which, in turn, will produce more information in sequences that tend to be terminated by information to which our responses are best described by the words "good" or "bad," "pleasure" or "pain." In some experiments with a mental maze that I did a number of years ago and that, to the subjects, seemed to be like asking them to solve an insoluble problem, the interpolation of the word "good" after the first correct choice made it almost impossible for them to solve the maze. They constantly returned to the situation in which the reward was offered, and took a significantly longer set of trials to learn the problem than the group for whom the word "good" was given at the end of the maze.

We not only process information, which is what our sensations, perceptions, and cognitions comprise. We process it in such a way as to enhance that kind of information which makes us feel good and minimize what makes us feel bad. The fact that we may often fail to produce pleasurable circumstances by our behavior is irrelevant to the general principle. It is equally irrelevant that some regard pain as pleasure. Only a fool, a madman, or a hero persists in behavior without hope of reward. In the old Greek legend, if Sisyphus, who was condemned in Hades to roll a heavy boulder up a hill, which immediately rolls back to the bottom so that he can roll it up the hill again, would just walk away, all of Hell would fall.

The processing of information to enhance positive states leads to a further perception of order in the way in which things happen. The way in which we function is to impose order on events. Anyone can demonstrate this very easily by setting up a random complex display of lights and playing music while watching it. In a very short time the lights will seem to change and move in accord with the music. If another piece of music is substituted, the lights will seem to accord with that as well. You can get some of the same effect by watching tropical fish in an aquarium that seem to be moving and swimming in time to the music.

We are an order-imposing organism. Most of us find disorder unpleasant, chaotic conditions unsettling. In the creation myths the world arises as the emergence of order from chaos. In most places, you can be arrested for being a disorderly person, but a devotion to law and order is regarded as a public good. The entire enterprise of science is the imposition of order on the flux of events. This is so important that data which question pre-existent orderings of the world are often suspect and may even be set aside and forgotten, as Charles Fort has demonstrated. If you have not looked at any of Charles Fort's writings, take a look at the *Book of the Damned* (Gordon Press). The Damned are the data that science and scientists—science itself doesn't do anything—have ignored because they didn't fit into anything. In our personal lives as well, we look at things with old eyes and mostly see what we expect to be there unless by some lucky or unlucky chance, something really pokes us in the eye.

Not only do we impose order on the flux of events; we also assume that what we perceive must be the way we perceive it. The Heisenberg principle in physics, which fundamentally asserts that what we perceive is a function of the instrument by which it is perceived, is a statement to the contrary and has had far-reaching consequences for modern physics. Most of us do not behave as if we believe we were subject to it, and we generally assume that everybody perceives things in much the same way. For instance, although many of us here are nearsighted, the idea that this is a condition with major effects on behavior rarely occurs.

Experimental psychology—at least modern experimental psychology—has been around since 1872, and people have been concerned with many of the various kinds of perceptual disabilities and their effects. As far as I have been able to ascertain, this common condition of nearsightedness was not studied experimentally until I carried out the first experimental study in 1965. In these experiments we artificially produced nearsightedness in normally sighted people by hypnotizing them. The hypnotically induced nearsightedness produced major changes in behavior. Not only was vision changed but also conceptual style, manner of socialization, mood, and perception in other non-visual modalities. You can get some sense of what nearsightedness does if you ask nearsighted people what the world is like for them. If you ask this, you will get some very interesting phenomena. You'll learn that social situations may be a problem when they're not wearing glasses, because they have problems in delineating expressions on people's faces. For many of them who were nearsighted from childhood, the experience of the first set of glasses was very anxiety-provoking because everything was too clear, too sharp.

Many people who are nearsighted need to wear glasses in order to hear voices on the telephone. A friend of mine recently came back from a week of meditation and in order to enhance her meditation sat without glasses, because she automatically didn't hear noises and other things that were disturbing other people around her. In such places as gymnasiums and indoor swimming pools in which people don't normally wear glasses, a strong minority of nearsighted people report that sounds get lower and louder, and they either become anxious or depressed.

On the basis of a report of a friend of mine, that when he and his wife have an argument he insists on her wearing her glasses, since otherwise she's crazy, we took a group of Princeton students and a group of students at the University of Oshkosh with 20-70 vision, or worse, and gave them—to the Princeton group, a special personality questionnaire; to the

Oshkosh group, the Minnesota Multiphasic Personality Inventory. When individuals with vision in the 20–70 range, or worse, answer the MMPI according to the way they feel when they don't have their glasses on, they produce psychotic profiles. Their profiles are normal when they answer it according to the way they feel when they are wearing glasses. Normal people with normal vision don't show these phenomena.

It's likely that if we were to investigate other kinds of perceptual anomalies, we could draw up a similar list of effects for other perceptual disorders. As none of us have identical perceptual apparatuses, no one of us perceives things in quite the same way, although we agree enough to permit intersubjective verification of at least those perceptions which refer to events that are out in the world. You can't, on the other hand, get intersubjective verification of such statements as, "I have a stomachache," because I am the only one who can feel my stomach ache.

For mind, the fundamental injury is to lose consciousness. If you know people who are subject to seizures, it's the loss of consciousness that they fear most. For a period to elapse in which data have not been gathered impairs the entire task of information-processing. While sleep is generally an acceptable hiatus, one of the common causes of insomnia is an endless fussing with data that will not be put away. The usual way of dealing with this in the commonsense area is to have you fuss with other boring data, like counting sheep. But this is still a fussing with data and often doesn't work very well. The poetic parallel between sleep and death doesn't arise fortuitously. Those who are fearful, those who are hard-driving, those who are overwhelmed with problems, have trouble sleeping no matter how much they may desire to do so. Sleeplessness is often the price of vigilance.

Closely related to the loss of consciousness is the presence of false perceptions, or hallucinations. While illusions, the kinds of false perceptions that are not intersubjectively verifiable, cause no concern since everybody else shares them by the way the world is structured, non-verifiable false perceptions are reacted to with concern bordering on horror. A fairly common complaint among many neurotics, and among some who do not otherwise appear neurotic, is the fear of insanity. Each person's concept of insanity is different. One may fear his own violence, another his own dependence. Common to these is the fear of loss of control, being vulnerable, not knowing what you're doing, not remembering, losing consciousness of what is going on. The image of death once more appears, but now insanity is a little death.

The association of not remembering with other activities often produces resistance to engaging in those activities. Among college students, this resistance is often associated with a long history of people following after you saying, "Don't forget or you will be stupid." Even where this history does not exist, most of us don't like situations in which we do not remember what happened.

One of the sources of resisting to be hypnotized comes precisely because many people believe that when they are hypnotized they will not remember what's happened. This isn't true; it is true only to the extent that you expect it to be true. Once this association is broken, previously resistant subjects often have no problem whatever, manifesting phenomena characteristic of the deepest or somnambulistic states of hypnosis. But first you have to convince them.

In any situation you have to forget a great deal. If, while I am speaking to you here, you were to sit and think of the name of the capital of Finland, you wouldn't hear a thing I said. The capital of Finland is Helsinki, for those who are worried. Unconsciousness may be chosen in preference to profound pain, but this is a special condition of balancing off adversive circumstances. The development of local anesthesia which permits consciousness to be retained without pain is a special expression of a fear of not knowing. It isn't at all surprising in the light of this that an accepted alternate way of referring to altered states of consciousness is to call them states of heightened awareness, even though consciousness may be equally profoundly altered by substances and activities yielding diminished awareness. Consider, for instance, the effect of the fifth martini on your state of consciousness in or out of a cocktail party. And alcohol is principally a drug for reducing awareness.

Yet, from time to time, some other person, or some animal —we don't usually apply this criterion to plants—stops moving and seems different. I remember when my miniature poodle, a dog much loved by all of us in my house, ran in front of a car and was killed. I remember how heavy he was to lift, although clearly in lifting him I was also lifting my own grief. We use the expression "dead weight" to mean absolute weight, or to express the sense that something is very heavy. There does seem to be a change when something dies, a loss of spirit, a loss of dynamic tension, a subtle change, which signifies that death has come. That which moved, behaved, and processed data now has stopped. Our only intrapersonal experience against the background of which this has occurred is that of temporary losses of consciousness. None of us, in this room, at least, has lost consciousness permanently. On the basis of this particular kind of past experience, it's easy for us to develop the sense of some kind of return to life.

Moreover, these formerly alive organisms eventually break down and begin to smell bad. Even plants will do this. Smell is one of the fundamental avenues of data through which judgments of noxiousness are made. The successful use of a noxious scent as a defense by the skunk is an excellent example. It also provides further evidence that for some senses similar affective reactions prevail throughout the mammalian kingdom, at least. Skunks are so arrogant as a result of this defense that they are perennially being run over by automobiles which do not respond in this sensory modality.

The sense of smell is associated with the body as a by-product of its activities, as well as with its excreta. This smelly envelope with its secretions, excretions, and corruption may

die, but surely not mind—surely not mind itself—which by definition even stands outside the data that it processes. We speak
of "my mind." Where are you when you are speaking of my
mind? Where are you when you are speaking of my body?
The mind, which stands apart from body and controls it, van-
ishes when the body corrupts and decays. It is not part of that
corruption. Reasoning by analogy, God, the ultimate data proc-
essor, is spirit, and not a part of the universe he inhabits, or
else he is a part in the same way and to the same degree as
mind is associated with body. In the Christian doctrine, "The
Word became flesh and dwelt among us."

Among the ancient Jewish cabalists, sparks of the Divine
Spirit were seen as trapped in a nexus of matter and seeking
to return to the source from which they were separated. In
Hinduism, creation results in three kinds of energy called
gunas, the heaviest and most material of which is called
tamas, and associated with foul smells and corruption among
other things, and is also characteristic of the lowest castes in
society—the untouchables. This is one reason that is given for
the caste system.

Of the Four Noble Truths of Buddhism which deal with the
causes of suffering from which one seeks relief by embracing
the Buddha Way, three—old age, sickness, and death—are
aspects of the corruptibility of matter. In fact, in Hinayana
Buddhism, one of the meditations is to sit around and think
about how loathesome your body is. The first of the Four
Vows of a bodhisattva in Mahayana Buddhism, which is,
"Wherever there are sentient souls to save I vow to save them,"
reflects a concern with similarly separating spirit from matter
so that karma, or cause-effect being, can end. On the other
hand, in the Mumonkan, which is one of the great collections
of koans, or questions, with which a Zen student may have to
deal, it is told that for saying that a Zen master is not subject
to the laws of cause and effect, one particular Zen master
spent five hundred lives as a wild fox, which is nice if you like
the great outdoors.

Over all, however, the stance of most of the major religions has been to regard matter as gross, and spirit as fine. The goal has been to punish human impulses and asceticize the body into purity. Many of you will remember in Dostoevsky's *The Brothers Karamazov* the shock engendered when the saintly Father Zossima died and his body began to smell. How could he be a saint and smell? In the introduction to *The Autobiography of a Yogi,* by Paramahansa Yogananda (Orientalia), one line of evidence presented for this particular Yogi as having been a saint is that his body did not smell when he died. How strange that a bodily mechanism, the data carried in the sense of smell, should lead to the conclusion that the body is vile. On the other hand, this isn't the whole story.

In Christian, Jewish, and Muslim belief, in the end there is the resurrection of the body. Men whom God especially favored, such as Moses, Elijah, Elisha, Jesus, and Mohammed, have all been taken up to heaven bodily. The resurrection on the Day of Judgment is a bodily resurrection. There is a distinct impression that without a body things are less blissful than they can be with the full complement of sensation that the body provides. Recently, as you were told, I was in Jerusalem. It is amazing to see the huge number of graves of eager beavers buried on the Mount of Olives, where resurrection is supposed to begin, so that they can be the first ones up when the trumpet sounds. Even if "out of the body" experience is real, it's nice to have a body to come back to.

The body represents, for most of us, a limit. We have intrapersonal events that take place, that none but ourselves can experience. We have extrapersonal events and interpersonal events that take place, that we can show. The body *is* an envelope, in a sense, if you will, for the mind. On the other hand, I don't know anyone who can adequately answer the question, "Where was your mind before you had a body?" The body *does* represent the limit of the self. I cannot feel beyond my extremities. Even though philosophers may argue that if every time you move a candlestick I have a pain in the arm, I would be justified in saying that I have a pain in the candlestick, nevertheless, for all intents and purposes, I have a pain in the arm.

We not only experience the body, we experience our bodies as ourselves. Every part, every aspect of the body reflects who we are, forms who we are. Major changes in personality can take place from changing the patterns in the body. This is the underlying principle behind such diverse approaches as bioenergetics, structural integration, and the Alexander technique. To understand how the body experiences, how we ourselves experience, frees us from reliance on external events. Often we experience the body as a wall, as a separation from other things, yet if we pay attention to how the body is experiencing, that wall doesn't exist anymore. When we were doing work with psychedelics in my laboratory, we sometimes had people come in who had discovered that they had had the greatest sexual experience of their lives immediately after using some drug—usually peyote, for some reason. It was a significant experience because they had become one with their partners. Everybody suffers from an existential aloneness. Most of us identify that aloneness with loneliness, even though they aren't the same, if you stop a moment to think. In the days following a peyote trip, apparently, these people, in the course of making love, were able to get into their body feelings sufficiently, so that they felt a sense of oneness.

The body is separate. The body separates only to the extent that the body itself is taken as part of a subject-object distinction. It is not I and Thou, it is I–Thou. The meaning of anything designated as a cause is found in its effects and there can be no causes without effects. The meaning of any effect is found in its causes and there can be no effects without causes. So that, in fact, there are no causes or effects existing independently of one another. The only way to talk about them is as cause-effect. There is no self to which to point apart from another or non-self, and the only way to talk about the self (not the way we usually experience it, because usually we build a barrier) is through the openness of self to not-self. In the mystical writings, this is called divine union. In the writings of the nature mystics, such as Wordsworth, you find a total identification with those events in the world around. Jacob Boehme talks about how he is the stone on which he is sitting. Indeed, this is the goal of at least one whole segment of religious experience, to transcend the self. The way to transcend the self, then, is not to use the body, not to separate the body from the world, or to use the body as a wall against the world, but to experience the body as one with what is impinging on the body. From the standpoint of mind, the body is, on the one hand, a perceptual envelope, or on the other hand, an envelope of responses for responsabilities.

If you've been around a hospital, you have seen people who are fundamentally vegetables, whose existence is being maintained because some idiot physician thinks that it's a good thing to keep life going even when there is no life. These are people who have no consciousness. I recently read in the newspaper of somebody who had been maintained that way for twenty-four years—essentially a corpse that breathes. There have been no responses to any stimulation in that twenty-four years. This person is no more alive than any stone—perhaps less. This is a strange definition of life. This is a strange definition of consciousness. This is not being one with the fundamental Void.

The fundamental Voidness from which we all emerge springs in the direct realization, the direct oneness, the direct manifestation of the self, the direct experience of the self. Voidness and direct experience go hand in hand. But in the final analysis, experience is what is central. Most of us develop systems to control and order experience. We create devils. If God were not conceived as all good, you wouldn't need a devil to be all bad. God-devil is like cause-effect. A good God implies a bad devil; a bad devil implies a good God.

Many religions, such as Manichaeism, which you may remember as one of Christianity's great competitors in the old days, believed that underlying the conflict between the Evil Principle and the Good Principle was a Central Principle. It was neither good nor evil, and both good and evil, and both good and evil as experienced by us in the world were the working out of that Central Principle. We impose external events. We set up the need to control from the fact that our minds themselves are based on control and order and thus we cut ourselves off from full actualization. Actualization occurs when there is a direct yielding to experience in all areas. Actualization occurs when you allow yourself to perceive without labeling, to feel without condemning. This is the true path of the mystic. It doesn't involve putting down the body, it involves getting into the body, enhancing bodily sensations, enhancing feelings, seeing what is there and responding to it.

In our present society we have increasingly been getting, in a sense, freer, but our freedom is very weird. It's very interesting that everything has to be a movement. We have the Women's Liberation Movement, instead of free women; we have now Gay Liberation, instead of the right to choose your own sexuality the way you want to; and fundamentally, the tons of manifestos that are written out of these movements miss the point. The point is that you have a right to actualize yourself so long as you don't injure anybody else. Because the fundamental principle is, and remains, and has to be, "If I am not for myself, who will be for me? If I am only for myself, who will be for me? If not now, when?"

In the final analysis, if I really believe what I'm saying to you, I shouldn't be saying it. The only way to produce this kind of message is through silence.

Discussion with Bernard Aaronson

Q: Would you define consciousness a little more? Would you say that when someone loses the ability to gather data, he is unconscious?

A: People who are conscious respond to stimuli. Therefore consciousness must involve this response. Since the only way you know that response is there is by reaction, consciousness has to involve the processing of those stimuli. Consciousness involves the processing of stimuli to produce information, the stimuli themselves being information.

Q: I've always considered loss of consciousness or fainting as a loss of control over my own activities rather than the fear of not being able to process data.

A: Well, that's the same thing.

Q: Is it?

A: You aren't in control of your activity when you have no data coming in. I worked with people with seizures for a long time. I once watched somebody have twenty-six seizures in the course of time that it took him to tell me that he hadn't had seizures for five years. In no case was he aware of any of them. A colleague of mine marked them down, and she had twenty-six marks by the end of that sentence. Now, he really hadn't had seizures for a number of years until it became likely that he would leave the hospital. He really didn't want to leave the hospital, but he didn't know that, so these seizures began. In a sense he didn't lose control over his activities, and yet there was no control, nor was he aware of what was going on.

Q: Would it be appropriate to describe the mind as the body experiencing itself?

A: If fear, anxiety, and the like live in the body, would you say that the mind is the body experiencing itself? It is that, but not merely that. How do you handle the fact that there is a beautiful rose growing outside? It has to be more than just the body experiencing itself.

Q: Where do you experience a beautiful rose growing outside?

A: It doesn't have a definite locale. You are the rose. When you asked that question, you were creating a subject-object distinction. In other words, suppose I ask you, "How do you realize a pine tree?" If you are approaching this from a non-temporal, non-ego self, you'll realize it by being the pine tree. That's input. That's stimuli. That's data in our sense. Normally, you would look at the pine tree; some people will bite it, rip branches off, walk around it. That's also data in our sense.

The aim is not to restrict the definition of how we relate but to make it broad enough. You can restrict the definition to such a point that you manage to exclude the whole of life. Language is a very tricky instrument, because for one thing a lot of people think it's real. There's nothing real about a word. A word simply refers to something. Once you restrict it, once you set this kind of structure into your head, you have difficulty transcending it, difficulty in having the freedom that was yours to begin with, and will be yours when a word is only a tool. So if you set a situation too narrowly, then you have to set up all kinds of sub-situations that will handle the other things you've excluded. Conversely, of course, if you set it up too broadly, you don't experience anything. A very good way of demonstrating this is by pointing out the way you hold a stone when you pick it up. If you pick it up just by allowing it to rest in your hand, you perceive very little of the stone. If you grip the stone very tightly, you perceive very little of the stone; in fact, all you get out of it is pain, if you grip it tightly enough. There is a place where, when you grip the stone, you are in contact and are relating to a stone. That's where your definition should be set.

Q: If we can process only a certain amount of information and data, and God, by definition, is not included in any amount of data, are we, thereby, doomed to never know God?

A: You do know as much of him, or as little of him, as you have the capacity to know. At this very instant, this very instant, you are manifesting God. You manifest the universe in yourself. All of causation comes right through you. If you weren't here right now, the whole course of the universe would have to be different.

III

THE ALTERNATING REED:
EMBODIMENT AS PROBLEMATIC UNITY

Richard Zaner

Professor Aaronson pointed out in his lecture that much traditional religion is in part based on a separation of mind from body. Perhaps more to the point, we could say, many religions often develop around the theme that flesh and spirit are fundamentally *at odds;* in their nature they constitute a radical *nisus,* a struggle having its roots in a kind of dualism. That kind of theme has as its deeply rooted philosophical counterpoint, especially for modern times, the extreme version articulated by Descartes, which grants ontological status to the separation between *res cogitans* and *res extensa.* During the past hundred years or so, there have been many and varied efforts to surmount the profound constraints such dualisms introduce into human life. Our categories of thought invariably work their way into our lives, and the dualisms result in still other forms of *nisus:* alienation and reification of mind and body, man and world. However, especially when it is a question of trying to *think*—or better, to *rethink*—human life and the human world, most efforts still occur within that dualistic framework.

A first formulation of my own thesis can be expressed in this way: if there is a "mind/body" problem, as it is often said, that "problem" is not "out there" as something admitting of a solution which, once reached, can then forthwith be passed beyond as no longer problematic, and business as usual conducted. Rather, we *live* that "problem"; we *are* the issue. As Marcel wants to put it, we are the stage on which the urgent problem is played out; hence, it is in truth not a "problem" but a "meta-problem" which is at issue. In different terms, I want to try and advance our understanding of what it means to be that exceedingly fragile reed, an embodied person, alternating between birth and death, between being and not being. What is this embodying organism by which I enact my life, or which willy-nilly enacts my life, through which my life is enacted and I am enabled to become—whatever it is I shall become? My concern is to try to show that the traditional Cartesian dualism, and any position that works from within it, explicitly or implicitly, is fundamentally inadequate to that issue, and in the end distorts human reality. Hence, my problem is to discover other ways of conceiving it.

1

It is probably, and if so happily, true that one need no longer recapitulate the seminal investigations into such phenomena as the "lived body" by major continental thinkers. The past few years have been remarkable for many of us concerned with such phenomenological inquiries. Although perhaps not entirely free from suspicion in all quarters, we no longer are regarded, to paraphrase Maurice Natanson's observation made a decade or so ago, as persons of dubious repute smuggling ourselves into polite society. More importantly, the issues which have occupied us are no longer suspect, as once they were.

For one thing, practically all the major studies of Husserl, Merleau-Ponty, Marcel, Sartre, Ortega y Gasset, and others have appeared in English translation, and quite a number of competent and serious critical commentaries have also appeared. Add to this the numerous journals, and the growing number of original works produced in this country, and the stature and impact of phenomenological studies is impressive,

especially if one recalls the marked lack of stature and hearing once enjoyed by those now recognized widely as philosophers of the first rank: not only such as Husserl, Heidegger,
Merleau-Ponty, Sartre, and Marcel, but others now sadly no
longer with us—notably, Alfred Schutz, Dorion Cairns, and
Aron Gurwitsch. Another generation of outstanding scholars
has passed, for the most part tragically, without the acclaim
they richly deserved. For myself, a public recognition of this
lineage is both a necessity and a delight, one that I propose
to acknowledge here by deliberately presupposing much of
their labors, by trying not so much to "go beyond" (Kierkegaard's pointed remarks about Heraclitus' followers, in *Fear
and Trembling*, being very much with me!) as to build in the
area their labors have helped to clear and cultivate.

2

My thesis can be put briefly: consciousness (or: subjectivity)
in general *is* only as *embodied by* that animate organism
uniquely singled out among the universe of other organisms
and objects as *its own,* and the animate organism *is* only as
activating or *enacting* that subjectivity. The primary difficulty
with Descartes's efforts to account for what he regularly called
the "intimate union" of mind and body—and the same holds
for anyone engaging the issue from within the Cartesian
framework—is that this very "union" could in no way be
accounted for by that framework. The logic and concepts gen-
erated from within the ontological bifurcation necessitates
what it makes impossible, as Pascal already saw lucidly and
with marked irony:

> Who would not think, seeing us compose all things of mind
> and body, but that this mixture would be intelligible to us?
> Yet it is the very thing we least understand. Man is to himself
> the most fabulous object in nature; for he cannot conceive
> what the body is, still less what the mind is, and least of all
> how a body should be united to a mind. This is the consum-
> mation of his difficulties, and yet it is his very being.[1]

The difficulty is consummate, for if there is indeed an intimate union of mind and body—if the mind, as Descartes says, is not merely lodged in the body like a pilot in his ship[2] —this can only mean that, contrary to Descartes's ontology, mind cannot be conceived as only "thinking substance," body as only "extended substance," but strictly and necessarily neither can be conceived without the other. To say of every entity that it can only be *either* "this" *or* "that" is false at best, and forces the consequently absurd conjunctive *both* "this" *and* "that" in the signal case of the thinker himself: although everything must be either mind or body, the thinker (man) is both mind and body. Neither the "either/or" nor the "both/ and" serves to make human reality intelligible, as Pascal saw; yet, as he points out with superb irony, human reality is inextricably mind/body.

My thesis can then be rephrased: to comprehend human life —i.e., embodied subjectivity, or enacted (animated) bodily life—requires a radically different logic (in the broadest sense), with its own conceptual framework and language, capable of expressing and accounting for that "intimate connection" or, better, *contexture*.[3] Gilbert Ryle's argument against what he calls the "dogma of the Ghost in the Machine" is in a way quite correct. Both "interactionists" and "reductivists" are guilty of that dogma and its consequent category mistake. To quote Ryle, since "the phrase 'there occur mental processes' does not mean the same sort of thing as 'there occur physical processes,' . . . it makes no sense to conjoin or disjoin the two."[4] The two sorts of statements are of different logical orders, and both the disjunctive "either/or" and the conjunctive "both/and" fail to account for the fundamental point, for Ryle. Namely, a person engaged in some action

> is bodily active and he is mentally active, but he is not being synchronously active in two different "places," or with two different "engines." There is one activity, but it is susceptible of and requiring more than one kind of explanatory description.[5]

However appealing Ryle's point is, it nevertheless involves a clear *petitio principii:* to say that "there is one activity" which, however, is describable in more than one way, is on the one hand to presume (not to demonstrate) that such statements, though logically *different* (they do "not mean the same thing," he asserts), yet can pertain somehow to the *same* affair; and, on the other hand, it fails to show what legitimates the presumption that there is indeed an activity which is "one and the same."

If one says that the action is "one and the same" because, after all, it is one and the same *person* doing it, that merely pushes the question back a stage: what constitutes the person as "one and the same"? More importantly, since the activity is presumably experienced and believed by the person to be *his* *fundamentally, his body,* what are the grounds for, and thus what legitimates the conceiving of, that "mineness" of the action (and the body)? It seems reasonable to say that, whatever absurdities his theory lands him in, Descartes had precisely this phenomenon in mind when he insisted on the "intimacy" of the union of mind and body—an intimacy which, I submit, is presupposed and not dispelled by Ryle's position. The supposed "ghost" merely returns to haunt the worthy exorcist. After all, Ryle still adheres to the conjunctive "and": a person is *both* "mentally active" *and* "physically active." He wants to deny that it makes sense to disjoin or conjoin the two, to be sure; however, he succeeds in this only by covertly readmitting the shadowy culprit of Cartesianism through the back door. Even if disjoining and conjoining make no sense, asserting that *both* "there is physical activity" *and* "there is mental activity" which perforce *must* apply to "one and the same" event, merely conjures up the same old ghost.

3

The issue which undergirds that sort of discussion is that of *embodiment:* in virtue of what is this particular body uniquely singled out for me in my experience, prior to all theorizings, as *"mine"*? As can be readily appreciated, the prime condition for there being an experienced world at all— hence, for inter-subjectivity, culture, history, science, and so on—is that in the first place I have this specific animate organism. Just as one cannot intelligibly speak of there being any visible things for the congenitally blind person, so would it be unintelligible to speak of an experienced world of objects, events, relations, and the like, without an animate organism through or by means of which such a world is at all disclosed, encountered, or experienced. Furthermore, in order for this body to be capable of being *my access to that world*, it is necessary that it *be experienced by me as "mine."* To speak of "the mind/body problem" is thus of necessity to speak of embodiment, and this in turn is to focus on "my body qua mine" as the *conditio sine qua non* for there being an experienced world. It is thus the phenomenon of embodiment which is perforce fundamental.

In effect, then, those phenomenologically oriented philosophers who have focused on the embodiment phenomenon have broken with the Cartesian ontological framework in order to rediscover and account for precisely what Descartes had himself come across without being able, however, to make intelligible: that peculiarly "intimate union" ("mineness") of mind and body.[6] That concerted effort has been remarkably fruitful, although its break with Cartesian categories has obviously required the development of radically new ones, with consequently different modes of expression. Thus in critically explicating the grounds for embodiment, Husserl stresses that this specific body (*Körper*) acquires the sense for me as not only *my* body but as my animate organism (*Leibkörper*) by virtue of its being, first, the locus of the several sensory fields through which objects and their various qualities and determinations are experienced as such by me. Second, this animate organism is singled out as uniquely my own because, in the course of my experience, the appearance of any other object turns out to be functionally correlated to the position, stance, and movements of my own organism. Most basically, the sensory appearing of objects is functionally dependent on the occurrence of what Husserl calls kinesthetic flow-patterns:[7] eye, head, arm, leg, or torso movements and bodily attitudes, for example, by virtue of which my animate organism functions as the *orientational point* from and on the basis of which objects are organized and arranged, displayed as "over there," "left," "under," and the like. Third, Husserl emphasizes that it is solely this unique animate organism by which my volitions, emotions, and valuations are most immediately actualized: my "I can," "I want," "I feel," so to speak, are expressed or made manifest first by means of my own animate organism. Hence, my embodiment signifies that this unique body is a *Willensorgan,* a *Wahrnehmungsorgan,* a *Sinnesorgan,* and my fundamental *point of orientation*—my "center," from which all order is constructed, hence in relation to which all "disorder," "derangement," and the like make sense.

In order for this body to acquire these crucial dimensions or senses, it is essential that it be a genuine system, or, better, *contexture:* it is an *organism,* that is, an organized system or context of perceptual fields, sensory loci, bodily movements, attitudes, and actional schemata. Somehow, not only do all these become organized as a totality (in the normal case, at least), but they are in some sense *experienced as such* by me, whose organism it is. The effort to probe that "somehow" leads Merleau-Ponty, for instance, into how it happens that this organism becomes a unified, synergetic system. With Husserl, he contends that the grounds for this totality are to be found in an operatively ongoing, *functional intentionality* (*fungierende Intentionalität*), an intentional arc whose fundamental stratum is inner-time consciousness.[8] Without any attempt to do more than hint at the very complex dimensions of such studies,[9] it is clear that one striking result is a definitive break with the Cartesian categorical bifurcation and its attendant difficulties. The systematic focusing on the "own body" (*le corps propre*) discloses that the mind (consciousness, subjectivity) is essentially *embodied mind,* and that the body (animate organism) is the principal *locus or enactment of mind.* Neither the "both/and" nor the "either/or" makes it possible to account for the phenomenon.

So "intimate" is this "union," indeed, that Marcel and Sartre are tempted to say "I *am* my body," and Merleau-Ponty that the "own body" is itself "a subject." To be a human being is to be embodied (*être incarné*), and this is pretheoretically, prepredicatively or precognitively to be literally "at," "in the midst of," or "with" the multiple objects disclosed and experienced by means of my own body (*être au monde, dans le milieu des choses*). The profound "union" of mind and body is such that it effectively constitutes an equally profound union between embodied mind and its experienced world. All divisions and separations are, in the strictest sense, subsequent to that complex totality: embodiment-in-the-world. Such divisions and separations are, indeed, for such philosophers, strictly theoretical constructions that result at once in a fundamental set of reifications, and in a serious alienation of human subjectivity from its embodiment and consequently from the world of embodied and experienced affairs. The result of such reification and alienation is that "my body" becomes "the" or merely "a" body; and in so far as "mineness" is essentially constitutive of "my body," such theoretical divisions result in this body's being eventually taken as in effect "any body" (theoretically, but also experientially, through such things as the stylization of body movements, the regularization of intercorporeal activities, and the professionalization of these in contemporary athletics). Hence, despite Descartes's evident grasp of the decisive issue—the "intimacy" of the "union"—the historical consequence of the slow elaboration of his ontology has been effectively the loss of that issue and a far-reaching degradation of the embodied, perceptual life of human life. The attentive effort to recapture the full richness of concrete human life, on the other hand, has realized notable fruits, only some of which have been indicated here.

4

Nevertheless, it is, I suppose, inevitable that with the exorcizing of old ghosts, new ones come to take up residence. Permit me to try and identify several, hoping not so much to dispel or demythologize as to pose them as crucial questions, enigmas which remain and must be accounted for.

Although it is true that this body is my animate organism (*Leibkörper*), it is as well a phenomenon having the sense for my experience of being a *body* (*Körper*). Not only is it the fundamental locus for my life and experience, it is also a biological and physical organism and *is experienced by me as such*. Whatever may be the status of certain concepts in biological science, medical practice, and the like, the "own body's" physical nature, or its "thingness," is not simply a theoretical construct. Sartre seems to me to have grasped this in his marvelous analysis of the way in which we experience our bodies as "being-for-the-Other": the critical disclosure of this ontological dimension, my being experienced by the Other as an object-for-him, is the experience of *nausea*.[10] Realizing that I have been "looked at" by the Other, I realize myself as a *thing*—as, somehow, physical stuff, caught or entrapped by the Other's gaze. My being-embodied, as the radical orientational point, O, around which everything is arranged and from which everything is experienced, is itself disclosed as oriented from *another* point of view—the Other's. That realization of one's own being-as-material, physical-biological stuff, is the experience of nausea. (The Christian notion of guilt, it might be noted, bears a striking resemblance to this encounter with one's own body.)

But there is much more to this. Whether or not it requires another's "gaze" (*le regard*) for this to become manifest, I not only concretely experience my own body as "mine," with all that implies, but, just as fundamentally, I experience it as *radically other than me*. Coupled with the "intimate union," in short, is a radical *hiatus*, an *allotriotēs:* a strangeness, or estrangement, at the heart of what is most intimate and familiar. For all the emphasis on the "mineness" and "intimacy" of this particular animate organism, which seem temptingly to persuade us that "I *am* my body," it seems equally clear that I am *not* my body, and this can be seen in the light of our concrete lives.

In the first place, to be embodied is, if essential, also *inescapable:* whatever may be my desires, wishes, hopes, etc., these must find not only their expression but also their radical *limitation* by the embodying organism itself. Like it or not, there are some actions which I simply cannot do, thanks to my having this and not some other body: "my" fingers are too short to permit my becoming an accomplished pianist, and I cannot alter that; I am "too short" to play professional basketball, and this inescapably. Even granting the marvels of molecular biology, with all its prospects for organ transplants, neurosurgery, etc., I am irrevocably determined in my life by the limitations of a body in whose selection I had no part, and which I must learn (and sometimes relearn) to move about, to which I must accommodate myself, with which I must reckon, in the nice phrase of Ortega y Gasset. And, even were I able to alter it, I in one sense merely exchange one set of limitations for another, and even then such alterations themselves are limited. Inevitably, the sheer passage of bodily time results in the establishment of corporeal patterns and schemata which at once determine and are determined by my experiences (with all their contingencies) and the course of my life. How I express my feelings is not only a matter of cultural determination; it is also, and more basically, a matter of which organism I have, and what this organism itself can permit.

Second, if there is a central sense in which my own body is mine, there is an equally crucial sense in which I am *its*—at its disposal or mercy, if you will. It has its own nature, functions, structures, and conditions; being embodied thus *implicates* me in these. I am of necessity exposed to whatever can influence, threaten, or benefit, my physical body: under certain conditions, it can fail me, not be capable of doing what I want done, force me to turn away from what I am engaged in and attend to it (e.g., because of fatigue or hunger, disease or injury, etc.). Hence, my body, despite its "intimacy," is as well the ground for frustration, anguish, pain, fears, dread, death. In this sense, my embodiment is a kind of chilling experience: whatever can happen to material things, can happen to my body, hence to me. Organic, physiological, neurological malformations or malfunctions, and the like dramatically manifest this implicatedness to me, whether or not any Other "gazes" at me.

Third, it becomes apparent as well that my own body includes events, processes, and structures which "go on" quite of their own accord, whether or not I am, or can become, aware of them. Deeply familiar, it is at the same time veiled and obscure. Indeed, it is solely thanks to such automatically ongoing processes that I am at all aware of anything else— yet just these seem to escape my efforts to know them. If I succeed in becoming aware, in my own case, of my heartbeat, this is itself conditioned by still other processes, thanks to which the first awareness is possible. In its nature, that which embodies my experience of things, that through which I enact my thoughts and desires, itself seems to be hidden from me. My own body is an alien presence (*allotrios:* strange, foreign), something radically *other* than me yet *mine* most of all (think, most simply, of when one's foot "falls asleep" and won't move as one wants it to; or, more critically, think of when—in Tolstoy's story—Ivan Ilyich is forced to contend with whatever it is that has gone wrong with his body).

Fourth, my own body thus appears as fundamentally strange. Whatever I may wish, *I* irrevocably "grow older," "become tired," "become ill," "feel energetic," by virtue of my own body. It has its nature, its own rhythms, and I find myself, so to speak, "in charge of" or "responsible for" something with which I must come to terms, which I must care for, whose functions require my attention—in short, which is in my charge, in spite of myself, however inescapable, material, chilling, alien, intimate, frustrating, odd, comfortable, disquieting, my own body may be to me. Responsible for it, I am at its disposal just as much as it functions to express and embody me. Compellingly mine, it is yet radically other: intimately alien, strangely mine. Most of all, my body is the embodiment of that most foreign of all things—death. In some sense, I, too, die; my body takes me with it, even to the darkness of elemental not-knowing—glimpses of which I catch in such experiences as sickness, injury, and the like.

5

Thus, whatever it may be that is designated by the personal pronoun "I," it turns out, as Julián Marías says, to be "literally *something other* than *its* organism—so much *other*, that it is not a thing but a *person*." [11] At the same time, we may say, so other is this "person" that its own body is not that person but precisely a biological organism. I mean: the basis for the otherness of "my own body" is its *having a life of its own* (or: its being-as-biological), even when I feel most "at home" or "at one" with it. Despite all protestations to the contrary, in other words, the fundamental enigma, which crops up in the very lap of the phenomenological disclosure of the grounds for "mineness," is the radical "otherness" of that very body, an otherness whose root is its inescapable, chilling, obscure, and strange nature as biological. It is at once both *Leib* and *Körper,* an organism and a material body, that by which "I" realize "my life" and which yet has a "life" of its own; an organism which, on the other hand, "I" shape, in which I govern, which I animate, and which is thus "informed" by me. So intimate is my body that I want to say "I 'am' it," yet my body seems to resist just that effort to identify myself with it, just as I distance myself, or find myself distanced, from it.

None of this discussion should, or can, be taken as denying the profound connections between subjectivity and body. My "I" is enacted in and through the body; my own body embodies me and my life. In fact, the intimate union is that only as contextualized by the radical otherness, and conversely. The truth of the Cartesian "intimacy" ("mineness") is found, therefore, in the *mutual determination* and *limitation, the reciprocal possession and enabling which are the basic sense of corporeal embodiment and psychical enactment.* In this respect, I am urging that we recognize the *mutuality* of this intimately experienced animate organism.

Beyond this, I have been trying to show that not even that complex notion of mutuality suffices to make explicitly clear the full texture and character of the phenomenon. The several illustrations on which I have drawn point to a still greater complexity: the radical *otherness* that is as fundamental as the *union,* indeed that *is* the sense of that "union." It has already been shown that the "both/and" and the "either/or" of necessity fail to do justice to the mutual fundamentality of otherness and union. One might be tempted, as I have been, to interpret this as a *dialectical* connection: my being embodied is a temporal process going on without my having to think or even be aware of it, and it exhibits fluctuations, rhythms, and a unique swinging back and forth between experienced ownness and otherness. There are moments in which each of us feels the resistance, the heaviness, the density and thing-like character of his own organism—moments when one's wishes, thoughts, desires, etc., do not get enacted, or are more difficult to enact. Equally, there are moments when just the opposite occurs. But, while embodiment does seem to be a temporally rhythmed flux—in virtue of which one must say that one's own embodiment is never in principle a perfect union, however intimate it may be—it now appears to me inaccurate to describe it as dialectical, in any usual sense. Or, if it is dialectical, it is as well something more or different.

It is not the case, I think, merely that at one moment I "am" my body, or feel myself very much "at one" (*heimlich*) with my own body, and at another feel it as an alien presence (*unheimlich*) resisting me or forcing my attention. Rather,

I am inclined to think, even in moments of most intense union
—precisely when, in Sartre's terms, I "surpass" the body toward objects, forget it in being caught up in some task, and
so on—I at one and the same time am and am not my own
body. This point becomes clearer when one thinks of how one
can and often does marvel at the remarkable way one's bodily
organism "obeys," "acts" almost "of its own accord," as in the
case of an athlete, an accomplished actor, a surgeon, whose
body movements and attitudes seem so smoothly to execute
the task at hand. It is hardly uncommon in such cases for the
person to feel a genuine wonder at his own actions, sometimes
even during the action itself. On the other hand, even when
my body seems as if it were incapable of doing what I want
—when my fingers seem so clumsy on the keyboard—it is not
that I experience simply the alienness of this biological entity.
Rather, the very nature of such experiences is that, despite the
alien presence of my body, it is mine most of all, fatefully
embodying me—clumsily, smoothly, and so on.

6

Embodiment is a complex, temporally rhythmed and continuously experienced phenomenon. What is critical is to find
a way to make sense of it—that is, to find ways of apprehend-
ing and expressing it without distortion. Aaronson's point
(which is also that of Buber, Marcel, and many others) regarding the ways in which such concepts as "cause" and
"effect," "I" and "Thou," must be thought, shows the urgency
of finding a different *logos* for thinking. Earlier, I mentioned
that the understanding of human life requires a conceptual
framework capable of expressing wholeness, or *contexture*.
This demand is hardly a new one, and there are really remarkable efforts to satisfy it.[12] I find the work of Aron Gurwitsch
especially fruitful in this respect, although I can give only a
brief glimpse at the results of his study bearing most directly
on perceptual theory. Still, several passages will serve my purposes and help me to draw some tentative conclusions. Speaking of the sense of "Gestalt," Gurwitsch points out:

To account for phenomenal features displayed by constituents of configuration, and derived by the constituents from this very configuration, one must allow for configurations as such. In other words, one has to admit that *configurations have structures, organizational forms, properties, characters, and features of their own*. . . . Such totals impose certain conditions upon their parts which are constituents rather than elements. . . .

To be a constituent and, in this sense, a part of a Gestalt means to exist at a certain place within the structure of the whole and to occupy a certain locus in the organization of the Gestalt. The locus can be defined only with reference to, and from the point of view of, the topography of the whole. By virtue of its absorption into the structure and organization of a Gestalt-contexture, the constituent in question is endowed with a *functional significance* for that contexture. . . . The functional significance of each constituent derives from the total structure of the Gestalt, and by virtue of its functional significance, each constituent contributes towards this total structure and organization. . . .

Thus, Gurwitsch concludes:

It is the *functional significance of any part of a Gestalt-contexture that makes this part that which it is. The part is what it is only as a constituent of the Gestalt-contexture and as integrated into its unity. Any part of a Gestalt may then be said to be determined as to its existence by its functional significance in the sense that the part only exists in, and is defined by its functional significance*.[13]

In these terms, it is hopeless to try and conceive "wholes" as either "more or other than" their "parts," or as "the sum of" their "parts." A genuine whole, or more accurately, a *contexture*, is precisely the multiple, functional co-relationships of every part (constituent) to every other one, and would not be "the same" context at all were one to remove any of its parts. Both the "more than" and the "sum" conceptions emerge from a logic which allows for only disjunction and conjunction, but cannot account for affairs which are neither. Contextures demand a different logic (in the broadest sense), one capable of expressing that uniquely complex simple, the "contexture" (*Zusammenhang*: the "hanging-together-of . . ." which characterizes every connection, ensemble, whole, or context). As Gurwitsch shows decisively, the most elementary phenomena apprehended by sensory perception are "wholes" in this sense, and only by subsequent analysis is it at all possible to introduce divisions, separations, and the like. Hence, for him, it is necessary to recognize another fundamental principle of the structure of consciousness in addition to inner-time (which Husserl had emphasized): the "theme-background" contexture which he expresses in his central concept of the *"field* of consciousness."

I want to suggest that it is this *context logic,* whose features still remain to be worked out, that best captures the complex phenomenon of human life, and therefore the embodiment/ enactment phenomenon. Expressed in one way, we can say that the *mutuality* of determination, limitation, possession, and enabling pertaining to embodiment is at bottom a *lived contexture:* embodiment is precisely a contextual phenomenon, a complex texture of multiple interlaced connections and reciprocal relationships. Thus, "the mind" is essentially inconceivable apart from "the body," and conversely—which is just what Pascal shows that the Cartesian was incapable of making intelligible. More particularly, just as the removal of a "part" of the body must inevitably limit the possibilities of action, desire, or what is enabled to be enacted, so too must the inability to think (dream, recollect, fantasy, conceive, feel, want, etc.) inevitably limit and determine the possibilities of bodily attitudes and movements.

I have merely scratched the surface of this veritable iceberg, but it already becomes clear how far-reaching it is. Permit me to conclude by suggesting several other features of this problem. Embodiment is a phenomenon of experience; I "live" it, which means that embodiment is an essentially temporal flux continuously expressing my "I" (linguistically, physiognomically, etc.). Hence, the contexture is essentially one that *becomes*, is continually becoming. A static conception of context will not do, but neither is it correct to say that its temporal becoming is merely a linear development. Certain features of both subjectivity and organism can and do cease becoming, grow in jumps and starts, lie dormant then recommence; others can and do break down and either become repaired or remain broken and different features develop. Hence, although embodiment is a contexture, it is a *lived* contexture.

Beyond this, that contexture formed by body and subjectivity is always and essentially "in the world," and thus necessarily mutually determined, limited, and enabled by that even greater complex system of interlacing connections. Indeed, the body-mind contexture is itself an *abstraction;* it is in truth "part" of that broader context which might be termed "mundaneity": *consciousness, animate organism and world constitute an integral whole,* precisely in Gurwitsch's technical sense, and just this is what the concept of "intentionality" means fundamentally. In these terms, it is by no means necessary to deny the possibility of focusing one's attention on one or another "part" of this "whole"; however, it is always necessary to recognize that such a focusing is a kind of abstraction (more technically, a thematizing or objectivating). The basic point is that one always has to do with "parts" that are *distinguishable but, strictly speaking, inseparable.* To pretend otherwise is to court that kind of disaster which we have come to know as reification and alienation.

Finally, it seems to me that the notion of embodiment as a lived contexture requires not only the notion of *mutuality* of interrelationships (intimacy, mineness) but also that of *otherness.* I am at a loss for a better term, but perhaps what I have in mind can be expressed this way. As opposed to any other kind of "whole," that expressed by "mundaneity" (and, with that, by "embodiment") shows a singularly remarkable feature: I am myself not only "part" of that mundane "whole," but *am reflexively aware,* and sometimes cognizant, of it and of myself *as* a "part" of it, and thus I am *distanced* from it. Moments of what might be called corporeal alienness (when I sense the radical otherness of my own body) might be understood as corporeal manifestations, having their own emotive texture (joy, disgust, etc.) of that unique reflexivity. In different terms, I experience the world of objects and myself as among them, I am an object in the world along with other objects; at the same time, I experience myself as the subject for whom these objects are objects in the first place. But beyond this *I am myself reflexively aware of myself as being both a worldly object and a subject for whom objects are objects—and this reflexive awareness is itself a positive and potent phenomenon.* It indicates not another, simultaneously existing entity (*pace* Ryle) but, as Husserl says, the *transcendental status of subjectivity itself.* Kierkegaard, I believe, had very much the same status or dimension in mind in his classic and deeply ironic, if linguistically acrobatic expression:

> The self is a relation which relates itself to its own self, or it is that in the relation that the relation relates itself to its own self; the self is not the relation but that the relation relates itself to its own self.[14]

This odd noun clause, I am suggesting, is what is at the root of embodiment, of human life, and of mundaneity. We find ourselves as creatures deeply contextualized by bodies, by nature, by culture, and by history. In a way, our vocation is to enable that complex, deeply reflexive set of lived contextures to come to fruition, first through expression, but also through art, science, education, philosophy, and politics—and without distortion. It is in the twin tasks of discovering the genuine character of contexture and of human life that I find the most challenging moment of intellectual labors in our times—and it is there that the probing of embodiment invariably leads us, at all levels.

NOTES

1. Blaise Pascal, *Pensées*, tr. by W. F. Trotter (Modern Library, Inc., 1941), pp. 27–28.

2. René Descartes, *Discourse on Method*, Haldane and Ross edition of *Descartes' Philosophical Writings* (Dover Books, 1955), Vol. I, p. 118.

3. See Aron Gurwitsch, *The Field of Consciousness* (Duquesne University Press, 1964), esp. Parts II and IV.

4. Gilbert Ryle, *The Concept of Mind* (Barnes & Noble, Inc., 1950), p. 22.

5. *Ibid.*, pp. 50–51.

6. Cf. Richard M. Zaner, "The Radical Reality of the Human Body," *Humanitas*, Vol. II, No. 1 (1966), pp. 73–87, esp. pp. 73–81.

7. Edmund Husserl, *Cartesian Meditations: An Introduction to Phenomenology*, tr. by Dorion Cairns (The Hague: Martinus Nijhoff, 1960), Meditation V; and *Ideen zu einer reinen Phänomenologie und phänomenologischen Philosophie*, Zweites Buch, Husserliana, Band IV (The Hague: Martinus Nijhoff, 1952).

8. Cf. Maurice Merleau-Ponty, *Phenomenology of Perception*, tr. by Colin Smith (Humanities Press, Inc., 1962), esp. pp. 98–153, 410–433.

9. Cf. Richard M. Zaner, *The Problem of Embodiment*, Phaenomenologica, No. 17 (The Hague: Martinus Nijhoff, 1964).

10. Jean-Paul Sartre, *Being and Nothingness*, tr. by Hazel E. Barnes (Philosophical Library, Inc., 1956), esp. pp. 303–359.

11. Julián Marías, *Reason and Life: The Introduction to Philosophy*, tr. by Kenneth S. Reid and Edward Sarmiento (Yale University Press, 1956), pp. 322 and 378.

12. Cf., e.g., Husserl, *Logical Investigations*, tr. by J. N. Findlay (The Humanities Press, Inc., 1970), Vol. II, Investigation III: "On the Theory of Wholes and Parts," pp. 436–492.

13. Gurwitsch, *op. cit.*, pp. 115–116, 121.

14. Søren Kierkegaard, *The Sickness Unto Death* (Anchor Books, Doubleday & Company, Inc., 1954), p. 158.

IV

THE BODY AS INSTRUMENT
OF SOCIAL LIFE

*Introduction to Panel Discussion
with Gwen Kennedy Neville, Cecil W. Cone,
and John W. Gill*

Almost all of the conference on Theology and Body dealt with
internal awareness of the body, with how we come to know
ourselves as bodily persons, with how we deal with ourselves
as embodied, and with how our bodies shape our worlds. The
panel discussion turned to another side of the question of the
body in theology. It dealt with the body as the instrument
of social life. It is only by being embodied that we interact
and build communities; and on the other hand, the needs and
desires of our bodies, as well as our bodily differences, are at
the root of the terrible obstacles to community which always
threaten us, and never more so than today.

The panel offered three perspectives on the body as the
instrument of social life, from the many that could have been
chosen: "body" as seen in the roles of women and men in religion and in the church; "body" as an element in the question
of the relation between blacks and whites, and "body" as an
aspect of the question of sexual styles and of the question
of religion's attitude toward homosexuality. Gwen Kennedy
Neville addresses the question of the body quite directly, show-
ing how physical differences between men and women have
to be perceived differently by men, so that women may no
longer be accepted simply on men's terms.

Cecil W. Cone attacks the question of the role of the body

in the relations between blacks and whites much more in-directly. For relatively affluent people, the bodily awareness of hunger, the pains of inadequate shelter, and the physical awareness of oppression do not first come to mind when the "body" comes up for discussion, and the affluent give much more attention to sexuality as a bodily function. For those excluded from bodily comfort and dignity it is a different story, and for them a bodily theology has to be a theology of liberation, such as is being developed in Latin America and in American black theology. Thus Cone very appropriately presents the black religious experience in the setting of a discussion of the body in theology, as an indirect but very sharp reminder that a whole view of bodily theology has to deal not just with our internal awareness of the body, but with the sheer bodily needs of men and women in society. It is clear that black culture in many respects expresses a bodily freedom that does not surface so readily in WASP culture. It is equally clear that the voice of black theology is not about to address itself to the body in theology in terms of those aspects of feeling at home in the body that are suggested by the role of music and dance in black culture, but at the fundamental level of a fairer division of those things which the body needs for survival and dignity.

John W. Gill presents the issue of homosexuality and re-ligion in a much more directly autobiographical vein. He does not argue the pro's and con's of one style of sexual life or another, but simply presents a story of the liberating effect on himself and his congregation, of their acceptance of that style of sexuality which they find natural. His is a strong plea for toleration of bodily differences in the religious community.

Thus these three papers offer a much-needed reminder that a theology of the body has to deal not only with the indi-vidual's acceptance of his bodiliness but also with the ways in which we are joined in community and also separated from one another by our bodily existence.

W. A. B.

WOMEN'S BODIES
AND THEOLOGY

Gwen Kennedy Neville

I have been asked to present in ten minutes a definitive statement on women that will offset two full days of lectures about
male theology by male theologians. When they have spoken
of the body it has been a male body. When they have spoken
of God, they have spoken of a male God. And even as they
have referred to human beings and to humanity, they spoke
only of man and mankind.

As an anthropologist, not a theologian, I feel compelled to
offer a counter opinion on the nature of the species. Women
are more than an interesting social protest movement. They
are not a "cultural voice"; they are found in every culture.
Women cannot be relegated to one third of one panel discussion when the conference theme is *body*. Women's bodies
are half of all bodies in the universe. Sexuality cannot be understood by males alone. And a totally male theology can
never hope to have relevance for all the people.

In this brief statement I have attempted to point out two
factors which I feel are of central importance in the invisibility
of women throughout philosophy and theology. The first is
that in Western Christianity women's bodies are associated
with the flesh and the earth rather than with the mind and
the spirit. The second is due to a seemingly universal human
tendency to assign magical status to that which is considered

powerful and dangerous—namely, menstruating or childbearing women. Because of my own interest in cultural arrangements and social structure, I will deal with each of these as it is related to and affects actual behaviors and the social organization of church and society.

The Flesh and the Spirit: Women and Men

Women's bodies have been a source of embarrassment to theologians since the beginning of theology itself. Throughout the Old Testament women are assigned to the realm of the wicked and unclean. Eve is made the guilty party in the Fall; her sisters throughout Biblical history deprive men of their strength, deceive men into leaving the wrong son an inheritance, become harlots and temptresses, and in general lead men astray. Even in the cult surrounding the purity of Mary, in New Testament thought, Mary is pure and worshiped because of her *virginity*—i.e., her separation from sex and sexuality—and because of her being the mother of *Jesus*, a male hero.

The social structure of the early Christian era in Europe placed women within a cultural and family cocoon that prevented most from taking active part in the writing of church dogma. As a result, church dogma continues the traditions of earlier, even more patriarchal societies. In this dogma an all-male Trinity rules an all-male universe which contains also "women and children" as a part of a male's worldly impedimenta.

Our contemporary churches have not changed greatly, either structurally or ideologically, even though a few piercing analysts are attempting to break through the indifference and radically liberate church thinking on this issue.[1] The conference in which we are engaged is a pertinent example of the way men who are in charge of planning church events leave out women almost entirely—not because they are hostile, not purposely, but simply because they *do not notice*. Their male-oriented world views pattern reality in such a way that women are patterned *out*.

Case study: This conference lists seven planners—all of whom are males. There are twenty-four names listed as participants. Twenty of them are names of men. Of the four women, only one has a speaking part. The other three are artists and dancers who seem to be totally in charge of the "Body" part of this erudite discussion of Theology and Body! In total there are six hours of lecture time devoted to men; ten minutes, to women.

As if the above structural arrangements are not enough, the culture and language of the conference has also reflected the all-male point of view. Name tags were provided which fit into men's suit pockets. Women who participated in Sam Keen's body workshop were instructed in how they could "pull their genitals up inside them." Vocabulary in every lecture used multiples of *man, mankind, he, him,* and *his,* with only one rather strained try at "persons."

These are the kinds of issues that face women in the church today and in the total society. Without regard and without awareness, events are planned and carried out by people who don't even notice that they are discriminating. For so many years no one noticed—not even women—that this was going on. Suddenly women have become aware—over a long period in reality, but coming to a head in the women's liberation movement—that these kinds of very small things add up to very large things.

The very large central fact is that men are being associated in theology and in the church with the spirit, and women are being associated with the flesh. There are many ways of expressing this dichotomy: spirit and flesh, soul and body, church and world, good and evil, male and female. In this conference, it means that when we talk about theology we are talking about males, and when we talk about the body we are talking about females. It means that in Christian theology the spiritual values and the intellectual thought processes have traditionally been couched in male terms and done by males. Women, meanwhile, have been allocated a secondary role, or in fact a non-role, due to their association with the flesh, the very unclean aspects of human existence, with the earth and with worldliness.

Women in churches and religious groups have been relegated to those roles most closely tied to the body. Roles sanctioned for women in the church have included childbearing, child care, cleaning up after children, making family supper and cleaning up after the meal, nursing the sick, making funeral arrangements for the dead, and making arrangements for family reunions (which are, after all, to honor the dead). These are very basic life-support types of activities. Meanwhile, men preach, pray, take up offerings, serve communion, make decisions, read, and otherwise perform thought-related intellectual and non-fleshy activities. What better evidence is there than actual *behavior* that we have created this flesh-spirit separation?

Ritual Pollution

In the preliterate societies of the world a behavioral duality such as this one is related to the fact that women menstruate and bear children, both of these being earthly and unclean bodily functions. In preliterate societies and, certainly in our own, all excreta of the body have carried the aura of uncleanness and the taint of what anthropologists have called "ritual pollution."

Anthropologist Mary Douglas has written extensively on the idea of ritual pollution.[2] She points out that taboos and avoidances in all societies are rules that keep powerful, dangerous, or questionable items in safe places. Taboos and avoidance rules maintain order in the symbolic and sacred universe and act to reduce the dissonance that arises around certain unexplainable and contradictory activities. In the preliterate world some of the most powerful taboos are found surrounding menstrual blood and childbearing women, highly powerful and magical occurrences in a nonscientific universe.

In terms of ritual avoidances, women in hunting societies are forbidden to touch any of the sacred hunting gear or the sacred ceremonial objects because of fear that they will pollute these paraphernalia. In our modern world a well-known company that manufactures intricate transistor devices has a taboo against menstruating women coming into the laboratories because "they perspire too much." Strong magical beliefs and superstitions, fears of pollution and rules of avoidance operate to regulate behaviors even in a so-called scientific belief system. As another example, when I asked a man at NASA last year about the behavioral taboo against women astronauts, the best answer he could come up with was that it was "a question of sanitation." I reminded him that if women had been in charge of designing the space crafts and astronaut's suits, there would be no problem. We have done very well at designing ways to handle our sanitary needs up to the present.

Even the wording of his answer and of our folklore is amusing. It suggests that there is something "unsanitary" about menstruation, and one has to have sanitary napkins to make one sanitary. The terminology itself implies that there is something unclean and unnatural about this natural biological process. An event that affects half of the human race every twenty-eight days would seem to fit neatly within the category "natural."

Religious traditions, theological doctrines, and church belief and practices have contributed largely to the popular ambivalence and revulsion regarding menstruation and menstrual avoidances. Karen Paige, Berkeley psychologist, recently found in extensive studies of large numbers of women in controlled experiments that menstrual pain and discomfort are correlated most highly not with physical or other social factors but with the religiousness of the women in question.[3] Her research validates the suspicion many of us have had that the strong religious sanctions against any sexual activity during menstruation, against strenuous play or athletics, against mentioning the word except in euphemisms (in one-sex company), have taught women themselves to regard their own bodies as unnatural and unclean.

Like our preliterate counterparts, our society has forbidden women to touch the sacred ceremonial objects for fear of pollution. Women have been excluded from the altar, from serving the sacraments or performing priestly functions. Even though many denominations are breaking down the barrier, it is even today difficult for ordained women to find a parish church as a post. A strong taboo still keeps them out of the pulpit and in assistant-type ministries.

Ritual language reinforces these behavioral realities. We have all grown up on all-male hymns peopled by Christian soldiers and men of God, starring God and Jesus as He and Him in the Kingship or Lordship over all Mankind. We have listened to sermons and prayers that follow this male-oriented pattern including us *out*.

Women, Bodies, and Liberating Theology

It is in the situation of women that the basic division of theology from body is seen most clearly. Because of their bodies, women have been relegated to a secondary position within theology, within the church, and within church life. Because of their being connected to the flesh and to bodily functions, women are victims of a kind of symbolic segregation that goes on at all levels of society, invading even the outer reaches of science, business, and the industrial complex, which are in fact grounded in Western theological tradition. And, sadly but in actuality, theology and church behaviors have taught women to believe that this segregation and these avoidances are a part of God's plan for the world!

Women's liberation has brought us back in touch with our bodies. It has made us realize that natural functions are not unclean but clean, and natural, and good. Menstruation and childbearing, the right to have children or not to have children, are God-given rights; and perhaps most crucially, liberation calls us to accept responsibility to be in charge of our bodies and of ourselves. Women's liberation has helped us see that we can love ourselves as individuals. It is no longer necessary for women to depend on men for economic or emotional survival, or on male priests or male church people, or a male God, for that matter. Women are viewing themselves as worthwhile. For the first time in recent church history, women are willing to work with and to love other women without fear or competition. Women are willing to forgo the security of dependency on males and to reject the necessity of becoming like males in order to get ahead in the world. We have sisters who are for us and with us. In the women's movement there is a solidarity that gives rise to cooperation and to group action.

This is what women's liberation in the church is all about. It is a theology that includes body and frees us from antiquated taboos and ritual avoidances surrounding the body. If this conference is truly interested in combining theology with body, in dealing with the entire species and our common humanity, it is imperative that it look toward the women and learn from their new consciousness of themselves. It is a liberating theology.

NOTES

1. There are many recent writings in the group now being labeled "feminist theology" and "liberation theology." It would be impossible to cite them all. I will give a few of the most widely known representatives: Mary Daly, *The Church and the Second Sex* (Harper & Row, Publishers, Inc., 1968). Sarah Bentley Doely (ed.), *Women's Liberation and the Church* (Association Press, 1971). Rosemary Ruether, *Liberation Theology* (Paulist/Newman Press, 1972).

2. Mary Douglas, "Pollution," in William A. Lessa and Evon Z. Vogt (eds.), *Reader in Comparative Religion: An Anthropological Approach*, 3d ed. (Harper & Row, Publishers, Inc., 1972). See also Mary Douglas, *Natural Symbols* (Random House, Inc., Vintage Books, 1973).

3. Karen Paige, "Women Learn to Sing the Menstrual Blues," *Psychology Today*, September 1973, pp. 41–46.

THE BLACK RELIGIOUS EXPERIENCE

Cecil W. Cone

Listening to Gwen Neville makes clear why we blacks have had so many problems all these many years. I am going to give a statement on the black religious experience in an effort to put in focus what that experience is all about.

Black religion is the product of African culture and the cultural environment of the American slave system. It was created out of the encounter of African religion with Christianity. These elements were woven together as the black slave *underwent* a conversion experience in the presence of the Almighty Sovereign God. This experience provided the slave with a historical *possibility* for existence in a situation of contradiction. It opened up the slave's inner being, enabling him to discern levels of reality not known before. The Almighty Sovereign God became the very foundation for every dimension of the slave's life.

Having encountered the Almighty Sovereign God in the midst of servitude, symbolized in the auction block and the slave codes, the slave experienced a knowledge of the divine will and purpose for humanity that his suppressors could never know. The slave developed religious forms in accordance with this insight. Although his religion took on the outward appearance of the Christian religion as it was given to him by the oppressor, the essence of his religion had little to do with white meanings associated with Christianity.

The essence of black slave religion was not a set of beliefs or doctrines to be memorized, nor was it an ethical code of do's and don'ts that the slaves learned. Rather, the essence of black religion was a black religious experience. The slave's encounter with the divine in the midst of slavery and the consequent recognition of his sinful condition was the first step in the dynamics of the black religious experience. The black religious experience is a depth experience of the Almighty Sovereign God from way down yonder, emerging out of the crucible of suffering. It is that experience of the divine wrought out of the slave's encounter with the absurdity of his condition and his meeting with the Almighty Sovereign God in the midst of that historical reality. Reality for the slave in America, in a historical sense, presented itself as immutable, impenetrable, and impossible. In the midst of this awful situation, the Almighty Sovereign God forced himself upon the slave as a *highly exceptional* and *extremely impressive* Other —the Wholly Other—radically different from everything known in this world. He was the God of power, whose existence was more real and more terrible than the absurd situation of the slave's life. The black religious experience, then, is meeting God in the depths of the despair and loneliness of slavery.

Although the slave was in rebellion against the system of slavery, and his meeting of the divine definitely had political implications, this meeting was not, as such, a political encounter. To start with politics as if political resistance were the distinctive characteristic of this experience is to misunderstand black religion. In black religion, God, not politics, is the point of departure. When the slave met the God of radical transcendence in the midst of the extremities of slavery, it created in him a sense of his own limitations—the sense of weakness and sinfulness related, not primarily to politics, but to the wholly otherness of God. God's reality and power became even more manifest through the involuntary and transformative effect it had upon the slave who was *already* in an involuntary, but *non*transformative situation. This potency of the divine was regarded as sublime by virtue of its creative process. This creative process produced in the slave an experience known as conversion, the key to the black religious experience.

When the slave encountered the Almighty Sovereign God, way down yonder where the slave was at the threshold of death, the Divine forced himself upon the slave in such a manner that the slave recognized at once his own state of sinfulness. From this point onward, the slave was in the hands of the Almighty Sovereign God. After striking the slave dead, the Divine exposed him to a level of reality not known before. When the slave emerged from this experience he was a new creature, completely transformed. This event, which is so keyed to the black religious experience, denoted fundamentally a rather definite and somewhat sudden change in the dominant beliefs, attitudes, subtleties, allegiances, and aspirations of the slave. The drama of the conversion experience for the slave centered in the birth of a new selfhood. It is for this reason that the slave emerged from the event singing, "Looked at my hands, they looked new. Looked at my feet, and they did too." It was this kind of encounter with the Almighty Sovereign God that constituted the uniqueness of the black religious experience.

When the slave emerged from his conversion experience, he was free. And this freedom which he experienced signified that the slave's life was no longer determined by the slave system. It meant that through his black religious experience the slave underwent such a change that his life was totally committed to the Almighty Sovereign God. Because he was free, the slave sang: "Oh, freedom, oh, freedom, oh, freedom over me. Before I'd be a slave, I'd be buried in my grave, and go home to my Lord and be free." The freedom of which the slave speaks is the present reality. He does not accept the designation given him by the oppressive society. A close examination of this spiritual reveals that the slave is very careful in what he is not saying, as well as what he is saying. He is not saying, "Before I'd be a slave any more," or "Before I'd accept being a slave very long . . ." He says, *"Before I'd be a slave in the first place!"* In the mind and heart of this man of African descent there existed a freedom that could not be denied. According to his own understanding of the situation surrounding his life *he never was a slave.* Furthermore, death would be his lot before he ever is one.

The freedom that the slave experienced in his heart and mind was a product of the black religious experience; but it did not cause him to ignore his everyday life. Far from causing the slave to bury himself in the kind of religious faith that is escapist and narcotic, the black religious experience gave the slave the necessary strength, fortitude, and character to fight against the legalized form of slavery. That is to say, the slave's involvement with the Almighty Sovereign God caused the slave to experience freedom at once internally, while it gave him the assurance that if he participated in the struggle with the divine against the institution of slavery, freedom would eventually become an external reality as well. The outcome of such a black religious experience was that a majority of the slaves participated in one form or another with the Almighty Sovereign God in the destruction of slavery. This participation that led to the black grapevine telegraph system ranged from collecting information, seeking outlets, lecturing against the system, and plotting and planning, to outright rebellion. But the key to this whole business was the slave's encounter with the Almighty Sovereign God—a black religious experience.

THE GAY IDENTITY MOVEMENT

John W. Gill

Sometime within your life you have associated with a homosexual person. You have worked, talked, sung, or even cried alongside this man or woman, and you did so without the knowledge of their sexual orientation. Therefore it was impossible for you to discover the special joys and pains the homosexual knows in his or her life. I am here that your questions may begin to be answered. I hope we can be open with one another and that ours will be a time of true learning. Let me begin by telling you a bit of my background.

My childhood was not unusual. I came up through the elementary, junior high, and senior high system of schools, then went on to college, and was an English major in my undergraduate work. Then I felt the calling of the Lord to go into the Christian ministry. I attended Princeton Theological Seminary and in 1970 graduated with a Bachelor of Divinity degree. It was in my second year of seminary that I began to realize that I was a homosexual, although it had really been a part of my life for six years, and I had simply refused to admit it to myself up until that time. I began to go out with other men, and to relate with them on a closer basis. As I accepted myself as a homosexual, there was no question within my mind and heart, as there never had been a question, that I was still a child of God and loved by him.

When I finished seminary, I wasn't sure I wanted to go into the ministry—not because I was a homosexual, but because I wasn't sure I could hack a job that required twenty-four hours a day with very little pay. So, I took an internship at a large, prestigious church in New Jersey, and served as director of youth activities in that church for ten months. I loved those young people and they loved me. The position I held was to be made a permanent one on the staff, and it looked as if I was a front-runner for it. But the Lord had different ideas and, all of a sudden, I was spun around and told by him that I was needed in a ministry to my homosexual brothers and sisters who had been denied the knowledge that the Lord loved them too. To make a very long story short, I shared this calling with the members of the ministerial staff in that Presbyterian church. I spoke to the senior minister on a Monday; on Tuesday, to the personnel committee; Wednesday morning I was told in the senior minister's office that that was my last day of work, and that if possible I should try and leave town in ten days. I stayed fourteen days. They were very kind and gave me a four-day grace period. When I asked for the financial arrangement, I was told that if I was a good boy and admitted I was sick and sought psychiatric help, I would be paid the rest of the financial package that was due me. If I refused psychiatric help, I would be paid only half that package. I thought and prayed about it for quite a few days and came back to them and said neither option was acceptable. The only thing that I would accept would be total financial payment because they had broken the contract; not I. I didn't know if I could take them into court and I shared that with them, but I did say that I knew fifty screaming queens in New York City that would like nothing better than to be loaded on a bus some Sunday, come out, and put on a show on the church's front lawn they'd never forget. In two days I got a check for fourteen hundred dollars. I did not do that to be vindictive or to be vicious. I wish to make it clear that I did it as a Christian challenge and in Christian

love. Of course, they did not understand that I did not have
the money for the bus, and I did not know more than five
people in New York.

Let me go on to explain to you a little bit about the ministry of Metropolitan Community Church, the church I represent. The Rev. Troy Perry began five years ago with twelve
very frightened people in Los Angeles, California. In five
years we've grown from one group of twelve people to fifty-
five churches, missions, and study groups throughout the
United States, in Toronto, Canada, and London, England,
representing four thousand members and eleven thousand
friends, for a total family of fifteen thousand people. The
church in Atlanta began in January of 1972. In two months,
when we celebrate our second anniversary, our church will
have seen a growth of 50 to 170 men and women. Metropolitan Community Church's ministry is a total one, fulfilling
the spiritual, social, and physical needs of its members and
friends. Through worship, fellowship, and a helping hand we
seek to re-create the joy and excitement of what it means to
be a Christian—an emotion sadly lacking in many churches
today.

Many of you are studying for some form of the Christian
ministry or you are already involved in a ministry. I want to
put a challenge to you, and a burden upon your heart: that
your brothers and sisters who are homosexuals need you and
are calling upon you to stand up and to help them. I will not
leave out my heterosexual brothers and sisters. At this time
within the universal fellowship of Metropolitan Community
Churches, we have three happily married heterosexual couples
that are pastoring churches—in Sarasota, Florida, in Kansas
City, and in Honolulu. You, too, can reach out to your homosexual brothers and sisters. We need you!

Now that the commercial is over, let me get back to the
speech. When I was asked what I wanted to entitle this sharing with you, I said, don't call it "Gay Liberation." Call it
"Gay Identity." Because this is not a liberating movement.

It's not a movement of revolution. It's an evolution of identity within the homophile community. In the last few years
there has been a change in the homophile community. We
homosexual men and women are not just listening anymore,
we're starting to speak out! And let me tell you to whom we
are speaking and what we are saying. To employers we are
saying: "I am a capable, trustworthy, dedicated worker. I
have a right to work." To landlords we are saying: "I do not
throw wild sex orgies in my apartment with the intent of
enticing small children into my home in order to attack them
and molest them. I am a quiet, responsible tenant and take
great pride in my apartment because I appreciate it. The
reason I appreciate it is that I never know when it might be
taken away from me." To the organized institutional church,
homosexuals are saying: *"You lied. God does love me!* I am
as much a son or a daughter of God as you are. You have
judged me, cursed me, ostracized me from your midst, but
I do not hate you. I pray for you. I pray that God may remove
the growing cancer of hypocrisy that is slowly killing you."
To heterosexual men and women the homosexual is saying:
"You accuse me of being sick, of being promiscuous, and full
of hate—and you may be right. But whose fault is it? You
cannot share or understand the love that I share with another
person of my own sex, and you condemn me for it. Brother
or sister, that lack of acceptance is *your problem*—not mine.
I'm free of guilt, of phoniness, and of shame. I'm busy building a new, responsible, meaningful life for myself." And homosexuals are saying to themselves and to other homosexuals:
"You've come a long way, baby, to get where you are today,
but you've got a long, beautiful way to go."

You, the members of this conference, can very easily turn
me off and disregard what I'm saying, and label me an angry
young man. But before you do, I want you to listen to three
stories I want to share with you in closing.

A young man, three months ago, happened to see me and
two members of our church on television. He traveled seventy

miles from a community south of Atlanta to worship with us. He came every single Sunday. And then we were concerned when he told us that he had to move a hundred and seventy miles south of Atlanta, but he still came every Sunday and worshiped with us. He was so excited about this new religious experience that he had found in Metropolitan Community Church that he couldn't help sharing it with some of his fellow employees at his new job at a college in southern Georgia. Unfortunately, some of those fellow workers didn't share his enthusiasm. They shared this information with the president of the college, and he was called into the president's office and dismissed—within a month of beginning his work at that institution. He has moved to Atlanta, and, praise the Lord, he has a new job. And you wonder why I'm angry.

Three weeks ago after a worship service I held in my arms a twenty-five-year-old man who was crying because, for the first time in over twelve years, he was beginning to believe that he was a child of God and he was loved. He sat in that sanctuary and told me the story that when he was twelve years old at a conference with a group of his peers (six hundred of them); the minister of his church called him in front of those six hundred adolescents, announced to the audience that this boy was a homosexual, and hung a sign reading "Pervert," around his neck. And you wonder why I'm angry.

I wasn't here earlier to share with you in the beginning of this conference because I was in Indianapolis, Indiana. When I returned from business in California on Wednesday, I received a call from a member of the Atlanta church, now beginning a Metropolitan Community Church in Indianapolis, who said that when the church had met in a private home of one of the members, on Tuesday night, five people entered that house, demanded identification, did not show their own identification, searched the bedroom area, and treated these people as pigs. Those five people were members of the vice squad of the Indianapolis Police Department—coming into a church worship service. And you wonder why I'm angry.

I could continue and share with you nightmare after night-mare. When I get complacent, when I get satisfied, there is an Indianapolis within my life, and I begin to work all the harder. I hope and pray that through conferences like this and through our working together we can truly begin to carry on a ministry of Christian love—and that's what it's all about.

Discussion with Gwen Kennedy Neville, Cecil W. Cone, and John W. Gill

Q: At what point, and how do we reeducate ourselves? How do we raise our consciousness? What do we say? "Okay, we like gay people." "Well, we think women are equal." "And we think blacks are all-right folks." What do we do with that? How can you tell other people to deal with that? Or is that just an unanswerable question?

NEVILLE: A number of things are being done by women in the church that have to do with conscious action to change the social structures, not only the structure of the church but also of society and other institutions. At Candler School of Theology a symposium is running all year called "Female and Male in a Changing Society." Such a program would be one of the ways you could continue to raise your consciousness and become aware of what women theologians are speaking out about in different areas of the church. Almost all of the denominations now have a task force on women that is, in fact, attempting in various ways to facilitate ordination for women, promotion for women, entry of women into seminaries, women being elected to offices, and other ways that equality can be established. I think that women who are in a denomination that presently does not ordain women should not let this stop them from going straight to seminary and just trying as hard as they can to change that, as long as it takes. If there are enough women in seminaries, enough women out there wanting to be ordained, then, they're going to have to do something about it. If we all sit around waiting for the men to do something we all know nothing's going to get done.

CONE: It's fairly obvious that while the black problem has many things in common with what might be called the "women's problem" or the "gay problem," there is the other side of the coin where blacks are women and blacks are gay. Simply to approach the black problem in the same way that you might approach the women's problem or the gay problem sounds unpromising. If it were the case that black or gay men were accepted, in that man's world that you were talking about, Gwen [Neville], then it would be simple. But I don't think the black problem is quite that simple.

NEVILLE: In fact, the black question is the only one that actually represents a *cultural* voice at all tonight. The black people have a shared racial, cultural, traditional identity, but the other two categories (women, gays) really cut across all other kinds of cultural categories.

Q: *Psychology Today* has an article on black women's getting positions more easily than black men. Is that true?

CONE: Yes. And I might add that one of the ways the white businessman has discovered how to kill two birds with one stone is to hire a black woman. Now he has hired a black and then he can also count her twice. He can also count her as a woman.

Q: I wonder if you would speculate about how theology might change if the interest your voices express begins to have an impact on the theological community.

NEVILLE: I've seen some writings recently that refer to God as "He/She" with a slash in the center of the word. And why not? We should also substitute "person" and "human" for the masculine "mankind." This is very important. Anthropology is traditionally defined as the "study of man." I now redefine it, every time I teach it, as the "study of human beings." The same thing happens in the church in theology. We could use "human being" and "human" instead of "man" and it would certainly help.

GILL: One thing that would automatically come about if our voices were heard in theology, and theology began to change, is that an openness and flexibility would characterize our theological thinking—an openness and flexibility that has never been present before. Just that change, due to the acceptance of what we say and do, would be encouraging to me. As new voices are heard or as times change we would have a theology that would be open, cognizant of the change, and willing to move and flow with it.

CONE: No matter how much we may pretend that we think in universal terms or that theology is a general kind of phenomenon, it is, in fact, the reflection of ourselves. So we have to change before theology really can change.

NEVILLE: Some of the problems associated with ritual taboos and ritual avoidances actually may be tied up in translation problems. In Genesis, for instance, the translation from the Hebrew regarding Eve as being sentenced "to bear her children in pain," could also be translated "to bear her children in labor." This pain thing has gotten into our mythology of childbearing and has messed up many people.

Q: Changing vocabulary is not going to do very much to male attitudes. That kind of approach leaves me mystified. It sounds like women's nagging. What are the tasks that women can perform that are important to the values that our world needs today? An admiration of the business world? Are we just unisex or is there something special that each sex can bring? Of course a man also wants to say he is gentle and sensitive. Is there a role a woman can play to bring that out in him?

NEVILLE: I don't agree that change in vocabulary is a small thing. Our language is a direct reflection of our attitudes. The way we symbolize the universe is inherent in our language. The words we use transform "raw data" of reality into symbolic patterns. This is very important. It's what we say when we use male, female, or neutral pronouns, for all people. I think this is significant. What you're getting at in your question about special sex roles is the idea that there exists a complementarity in human nature. There are aggressive, hostile parts and gentle, nurturing, loving parts in the nature of all human beings. Our society happens to have ascribed certain character traits to males and others to females. The aggressive and hostile parts become male dominant characteristics, while the submissive, passive characteristics become female. That is a fallacy. Our society simply assigned those characteristics because it was adaptive for our society's survival to do so, and it kept the social structure together in a very good way. I don't think this designation is adaptive any longer. We need to redefine *human beings* as having these traits—some soft and gentle, and some harder and more assertive. These characteristics can be played out by either males or females, or heterosexual or homosexual people, with whatever personalities they bring into jobs and into roles. I think, for instance, that our male presidents have made some very bad decisions even without menopause or menstruation.

Q: It seems that women are put down principally because men don't want to share financial and governmental power in our system. Gays are put down because otherwise it militates against the masculine stereotypes, the molds that maintain the extant kinds of power relationships. The blacks are put down also. They were kept in slavery to keep a power system going, and they're kept down because those in power don't want to share their power with blacks.

NEVILLE: We haven't been using a power model at all. We've really been discussing strictly in terms of a symbolic model. So much of what has been symbolically stated in religious ceremonies and in religious language is supporting a power structure that, in fact, does have white Anglo-Saxon males at the top, in our culture particularly. This whole question may boil down, essentially, to a question of economics and control of resources.

GILL: I agree, but I think power is just a part of a larger picture. The *status quo* is the more important concept that needs to be considered. Women, gays, and blacks are especially threatening that *status quo*. The necessity to understand a woman in her new role in the world today, to accept the homosexual or the black, is something our status-conscious culture is not willing to do. I still maintain that it's because we are all afraid of ourselves and do not understand ourselves. No acceptance and growth is going to occur until the American public starts to examine its own life. But they will not do that, for fear of upsetting the *status quo*. For example, I firmly believe that of all the men in the world today the American male is the most threatened as far as his masculinity is concerned.

CONE: The center of that power behind the system is very small. The majority of the persons in this country share in that power only from a distance, but they are nevertheless responsible for the support of that power. Maybe it's because we love order and an ordered society and we have been brainwashed from the time we were small tots into thinking a certain way. The persons who really have the power in this country do not have to defend that power. It will be the persons who are out here who will defend that power for them. These persons who defend the power or the right for things to remain as they are, in many instances, will be suffering from a type of oppression from that same power base and not know it.

Q: In the United States we have a particular admiration for the military. I think Charles Atlas courses are needed so men can show their mettle. If you have served your country you are a man. If you have been in prison you may not be able to use that term. I can't separate our worship of the military, including church peoples' worship of the military, from all of these other problems.

GILL: A very wise Episcopalian theologian, Norman Pittenger, has stated that it's not a question of homosexuality or heterosexuality, it's a question of *human* sexuality that threatens us today. It's not a question of what is a man or a woman; the more specific question asks what is a human being and what composes that human being. This type of question exemplifies what we are afraid of today. In American society a little boy plays with girls when he's young, but when he's twelve he's pushed out of doors with a baseball bat and a baseball, and that's it! A father will hug his son until the son becomes twelve and then automatically there's no more emotion shared with that son. We have fallen into this pattern. From twelve on, you are labeled as a man or a woman and certain things are expected of you—instead of someone's helping you develop, and later on, your helping yourself to develop as an individual *human being*, not simply as a man or a woman.

Q: There is a common thread through each of the frameworks you are using to prevent this kind of discrimination. The common thread is that each of you picture your history as subjugation. The correction I hear being offered to this is your shared humanity. In the therapy workshop Tom Driver said that one thing we are very afraid of is celebrating our differences. One thing that is obvious is how different you feel your bodies to be. Yet the correction to subjugation has been in terms of what is common among you. What kind of answers can you give in terms of your difference, your individuality?

TOM DRIVER: This is related to the point that was raised about power a minute ago. There is no doubt in my mind that the movement that is necessary is the description of difference. How is it? What's good about this panel is that we've heard something about this. It's just like telling the news. That's where it starts. When you tell it you discover both similarities and differences. What makes you most edgy is difference. What's so wrong with me? What's wrong with you? There's an immediate feeling—something is wrong about difference. There are thresholds there and anxieties. But one can move with them and through them.

But the question of power has been raised, and that's what makes it a tough game. I don't believe that power questions can be dissolved into psychological questions. I agree with you, Gwen [Neville]. I think symbolism is terribly important, but it doesn't account entirely for the power struggles. The power struggles use the symbolism. Granted that there's probably going to be somebody on top, whom do they pick to be on the bottom? There the symbolic thing comes in very strongly. It's no accident that you three panelists are the shadow side of the American male. So, you've always got that business about what's picked for victim is shadow, the part that I would rather eliminate. Now, where do you go from there? Well, I'd be stupid to say that I really knew, but somehow or other, I think it involves a reunderstanding of what power is. That's where I think that the theological change has really got to come. There was a question about that a minute ago. How should the theology change? We need the changes in vocabulary, in symbolism, which are, indeed very important, making really the opening wedge. I think that there's got to come an understanding of power that is not cast in terms of dominance. At this point the Christian religion is, as we have received it, not good enough. For even though it contains the motif of suffering servant, he who surrendered himself, that suffering has always been cast in terms of his divinity, the servant had the privilege of counting himself equal with God, and so all the action is within the scenario of Lord of Hosts. I think somehow that framework has got to give, and I think what's going to make it give is pluralism.

V

SPEAKING FROM THE BODY

Tom F. Driver

I want to start with two observations: one, because I need to get it off my chest; the other because it will lead to what I want to do at this time. If Gwen Neville had not already done so, I would have said something about female participation in the lineup of this conference. We will not be able to shift our sights in the way we need without the full participation of female human people. We cannot get where we need to go on the topic of theology and body without female participation.

The other observation is that we have tended in the conference to hold the body somewhat at arm's length. That is what leads me to my choice about what to do with the time I have with you now. I will not hold the topic at arm's length, will not speak about the body, but, as it were, I will speak from my body. Yesterday Dick Zaner referred to Merleau-Ponty's use of the term *le corps propre*, "the own body." Already that definite article is out of place. It is not *the* own body, but *my* own body, and *your* body. The body is locus. I want to speak from my own particularity and do this by telling a story. One reason that I love Sam Keen is that he taught me to tell stories. But as you will soon see, he did not teach me how to tell them. You cannot really learn from somebody else how to tell your own story. I have to tell my story my way. I had to find out for myself how to do it and that took work. It is exactly that work that I would like to share with you now.

The theologian soaked in the bathtub. It had been a late night with old friends talking of religion and psychology until way in the morning. As so often in summer, the dawnlight woke him, though his limbs were still tired. He got up and looked at the fog hanging at the tops of the trees. It blocked out the sky and the mountains, a giant filter holding back most of the light of the sun.

Inside himself he felt foggy, too, yet restless with some old energy earth fathers. The house was still, its three other occupants asleep as well as the cat and the two Labradors. The house was large, a "summer bungalow" built in 1900 for a big family, some servants, and no telling how many guests. While it was not pretentious, its space and simple furnishing gave him a sense of luxury, as if the purpose of life were living, as if family life were a good thing provided there was space enough and time for each person to have some privacy. He turned his attention inward.

Tired limbs and untoned muscle spoke to him. "Wash us," they said. There was a chorus of complaint in his body. "Take care of me. Treat me with love."

He remembered that in forty-eight years and in spite of a deeply sensual nature he had never quite made peace with his body. It was one of several reasons why the knowledge had mocked him when he learned, long after growing up, that he was born under the sign of Gemini. Now his body, which at times was that "heavy bear" Delmore Schwartz made a poem about, was crying. If he did not respond, it might despair, grow sick, or (much worse) launch into a monologue as long and accusatory as the speech of Caliban in Auden's *The Sea and the Mirror*. He longed—or was it his body that longed— for the sea. "Wash me. Take care of me."

The house had five bathrooms, and his was at the end of the

hall. His bathing would disturb no one. The bathroom in his own summer house had no tub, only a shower stall. True, there was a swimming pool into which he would plunge once, maybe twice, a day. Yet there he tended to be rather aggressive, as in so much of his life, as if the purpose of living were to hurry. No doubt about it, and sensual as he might fancy himself to be, he had the disease of the Puritan ethic aggravated by technology and the media. Whatever he did, he wanted to do and be done with, the better to do something else. He would dive in the pool, get out, dive again. After several immersions he would splash a bit, churning the water. Then he would swim a few laps, get out, and dry himself, done with it. He professed to enjoy this, and you could hear him exclaim how marvelous it was; but he noticed that in the middle of his "dip" his mind had already gone on to the next thing, even if he did not yet know what that would be. He lived eschatologically, always for the end, although he had long since ceased being able to imagine an end of history or time, or even the end of his own days. Therefore, he lived for little, finite ends over and over, losing interest in episodes before their finish. He was good at starting and stopping—no, to be truthful, at starting and quitting, though he could often manage to end a speech or a letter with quite a flourish—but he was not good in the middle of the course. He had a problem with "centering."

"Wash us."

He went into the bathroom and filled the tub with warm water. Then he sat down in it and began to wash himself. The idea was to wash every part, to bathe and caress every section of his skin, as if his were the body of a baby or a sick person to whom he might minister with rag, soap, water, and gentle touch.

"Wash me, and I shall be whiter than snow. Purge me and I shall be clean." It was not a prayer to God but an instruction to himself. Still, there was something incantatory about it, and he perceived that he was conducting some sort of ritual.

Better, however, not to think too much about the known ritual of washing. His mind skipped lightly over the images of baptism, foot-washing, anointments with oil.

But these images were all too liturgical, too Biblical, and therefore too dangerous to his present activity. They might interpret it for him before it had happened, which he sensed was the error of theology—always knowing too much—and which reinforced his own hurried tendency to skip over the middle of an act. So his mind turned, for a languid moment, to Leopold Bloom in the bathtub, and he re-Joyced once more in the Irishman's comically gorgeous image of his penis floating in the water like a lily. Consider the lilies of the water. They toil not. Neither do they stiffen. Well, he had the gospel in his soul, and not even Joyce—who probably had it in his soul, too—would erase it. Where he seemed not to have the gospel was in his body, and he felt that if his body's longing for salvation could not be filled, then he had not the gospel at all, really. For he knew enough to know that the gospel was not an idea but a deliverance. It was therefore an act; and no act, not even an act of the mind, was conceivable bodiless. The gospel would deliver his body, or it would deliver nothing. Why had he never been told this? Once he thought of it, he knew it with absolute certainty: the fate of the self is the fate of the body, and the gospel is body-gospel, but none of his teachers had ever said so.

These thoughts rose in him and mercifully subsided. He returned to his limbs in the water. They were still waiting to be washed.

He started with his face, which he gave himself to feel. Lightly he followed all the crevices in each ear. When he was in a hurry, all these irregular shapes and turnings in the ear bothered him. They could not be washed efficiently. But when the ear is explored at leisure, as he had already discovered in times of extended foreplay with his wife, it takes on a mysterious beauty. Was there a correlation between this and the mystery of oral communication? We do not look at the ears of a person when we talk to them, hardly so even when we whisper into them directly. The message goes into this incredible crevice, this cavernous antenna, and we look for the response elsewhere, in eyes, face, and movements of the whole body. In its combination of creviced ugliness and beauty, the ear is like the vagina and its lips. He wondered, for a second, if he had any right to explore his own ear so carefully, to get inside it with the probe of his finger. The more gentle his touch, the more he felt that he might offend some intimate and ultimate silence. But the ear gave itself to his feel, and the barrier was crossed into warmth and reverie.

He proceeded to his neck, arms, and shoulders. Here the contours were broad, his instinct to love uninhibited, the same reaction to his own body that he had to others! He went on to his chest and stomach and all the way down. He washed his abdomen, his groin, his genitals with mild erotic pleasure. He washed his legs and his feet, and ended with the spaces between his toes.

To all this care his body responded. He could feel life stirring within him. His penis tingled, grew spongy, but not erect. It was in that state, so pleasurable to men, midway between flaccidity and frustration, a reminder of vitality without an imperative to action. It is a state of bemusement, not quite serious, not quite comic, and communicates well-being. He lay back in the water and smiled. He was happy.

In a moment it came to him that the ceremony was not finished. He could not think why not, but he was sure it was true. If he followed his usual way, he would put aside such a slight feeling of incompletion. Life is never complete. Don't dally. The bath is over. Get out, dry yourself, go on. But he waited. What was it that wanted to be done? The voices that had said, "Wash us," were still. Or almost so. It seemed as if one member of that chorus still made a murmuring sound. Not a word, not an entreaty, just a faint sound. Almost like a whimper of despair, yet hardly even that. Something wanted attention, but he did not know what, how, or why. He waited.

He lay back in the water and raised his knees. Then he reached out with his hand, touched his right knee, and moved his palm along his thigh. Then both hands, to encircle the thigh and stroke it all over. He did the same with the left one and realized he had come in contact now with a point of inner contradiction. No, the bath was not finished. More than that, something between his knees and his hips had never been finished, had never seemed quite right or completed for as long as he could remember.

The very word "thigh" offended him. He had been conscious of this some time earlier and had even mentioned it to his wife, who thought he was crazy. When she spoke of chicken thighs, he winced. The proper term, which he had learned as a child, was "upper joint." The word "thigh" reminded him of flesh too soft and skin too white. He had never liked photographs of women with their thighs exposed between stockings and garter belt. In fact, although he enjoyed erotic pictures, he had never been able to imagine how anyone could fail to be turned off by that particular costume, which puzzled him no end because the motif was repeated in men's magazines over and over. Most of all, he did not like his own thighs. In fact, now that he thought of it, his unconscious, his unthought habit of mind, seemed to deny that he had thighs at all. Legs, yes, but not thighs. Not in any sense of identification. If he went to the doctor about a rash, he might say, "It's on my thigh," but that was a purely objective statement. Indeed, he was more likely to point and say, "It's here." Something about a thigh he didn't like.

Now he continued to touch it. What was it he refused? Too soft and too white. Too much useless flesh. The flesh around his middle didn't bother him. True, his silhouette with the expanding waist was not attractive, but the stomach flesh itself felt good, and he liked to gather it in his hand. But not the flesh of his thigh. The sun never got to it, especially on the inner side. The fatty flesh of his two thighs sometimes rubbed together when he walked, which could not have been what

God intended. He had no theological belief that flesh was sinful, but this flesh was. It caused an alienation. Obviously at
this point he was alienated from himself. But that wasn't all.
The offending flesh was to be hid also from God.

What God had to do with his thighs, or they with Him, he
couldn't imagine. He searched his theological memory. The
only thing he came up with was the bit in Genesis about the
angel touching Jacob on the thigh. He didn't know if that was
important. He remembered some commentaries saying the
expression was euphemistic, that it meant the angel had
touched Jacob's testicles, because many ancient people swore
by their balls. He could hardly think of a more powerful oath,
but he didn't quite think in his own case that he had displaced
a shame about his genitals to his thighs. Maybe he had, and
ten years of analysis would prove it, but he was not now going to go on a bookish hypothesis that had no internal hunch
to support it. More likely that he had followed a child's logic
from hearing the Genesis story and had hid his thighs from
God so the angel wouldn't get to them and change his name
and his life and make him a villain-hero like Jacob.

This came a little closer, because he did believe in election
or religious destiny or whatever you call it, and if there was
something between his thighs or any part of himself and God,
it surely had to do with whatever he was supposed to become
in the divine dispensation. But even this, while partly to the
point, did not ring with full conviction. It was still too deduc-
tive, too literary an interpretation of feelings that were still
playing shy at the doorway of his mind.

The only thing of which he was sure was that his thighs
were a point of alienation. He had them in his thought as a
burden of sin. This was the craziest idea that had ever occurred to him. That is, it was crazy to take it seriously. But
obviously it was serious or he would never have dragged the
thighs of chickens into it. Nor would he have been blocked
in astonishment whenever his wife would say, in bed, that
the most delicious part of the body was the soft inner flesh

of the thigh. For a sensualist to draw a blank at such a statement, for him to be so perplexed that he couldn't even disagree
and could merely mutter a yes, yes, without believing it, was
seriously crazy. Of course, he had an easy out. Everybody
has hang-ups, and it's foolish to dwell on them. His wife had
long since taken this attitude, and while she knew he was
crazy in this regard it didn't bother her because she thought
everybody had the right to be crazy, except when he went out
of his mind with anger at something, which it never occurred
to either of them to connect with his thighs, since you could see
where his anger was, and it was in his flushed face, tight neck,
threatening arms and fists. He was soon to discover more about
this anger, but right now he was making some first, tentative
connections with unknown territory.

The alienation in or from his upper legs had gone on so
long that in the normal course of things the most he could be
aware of it was the vague sensation of an inner despair if it
made any sense to think of a despair in one's leg. He carried
sin in his flesh. He carried his sin in the rejected flesh of his
thighs, which flesh, unused, unattended, unloved, had ever-
more lost its tone. It was—he tried to avoid the thought—
carrion.

He wondered if he believed in original sin. This was, for
the modern mind, the most offensive of all Christian doctrines,
and he was certainly offended by it. He tended to agree with
the French philosopher, Paul Ricoeur, that it is a pseudo doctrine, a piece of myth dressed up as a rational thought. Original sin meant that you were born wrong, so that you couldn't
do anything really right. And this condition was inherited,
one generation from another, all the way from Adam and Eve.
He had no truck with Augustine's version, which was that the
sin was transmitted through the lust of the sex act in which
we are conceived. Nor did he believe in the doctrine for the
good Christian reason that it postulated the disease for which
Christ was the cure. You ought not to invent a complaint in
order to justify the remedy. The worst thing wrong with the

doctrine was that it stood in the way of one's affirming the goodness of self, neighbor, and nature. Regarding self and neighbor, to be sure, original sin warned you not to be surprised when people did evil things, and this forewarning could lead to a certain charity of mind, as he had learned long ago from Reinhold Niebuhr. But the problem didn't lie at this moral level. It lay deeper, at a level his teacher Paul Tillich would call ontological, and which he himself called the level of faith and celebration. Any doctrine that clouded or inhibited the natural joys of existence was itself sinful, for it precluded spontaneous praise. Orthodox Christianity had therefore become crabbed. It could praise God for what he did an aeon ago on the first day of creation, for what he did in the so-called gift of his so-called begotten Son, and for what he would do at the end of time. It might even praise him for his providential control of history. But Christianity knew nothing of how to praise God, or anything else, for the sheer joy of it. It was the Calvinists, no less, who had been smart enough to say that "the chief end of man is to glorify God, and to enjoy him forever"; but Calvinism itself was joyless. Instead of taking pleasure, it seemed only to hope that the time will come when it might do so with a clear conscience. This was the dour fruit of the doctrine of original sin, and the theologian rejected it for that reason. Whatever sin meant, it did not mean that the goodness of God and creation are at some necessary remove from us until the end of time. Nor that our only foretaste of it is mediated through the Christ. In fact, the only problem for Christianity lay in this tendency to think that goodness is mediated. On the contrary, he thought, goodness is immediate and evil is mediated. Evil arises from the interposition of something between the self and its own life. It had been a dreadful mistake ever to call sin original. Far from being original, it is a perversion. These thoughts tumbled through his mind. They were true enough, but not sufficient. They were things he had more or less sorted out in the past. But if he now began to think inductively from the starting point of the sin in his thighs, he reached a somewhat different conclusion. The experience of his own alienated flesh led him to reflect upon his own personal past. What was the history of these thighs that seemed as if somehow stuck in a previous time, reluctant to join the rest of his body in the present? He had come upon an obscurity, and something beckoned him to trace it through an obscure past. The evil, whatever it was, stood between the past and the present, blocking the flow of time. He would have to wade upstream and find the place where the fallen log, or maybe a beaver dam, had impeded the current of the waters.

His mind flashed back to a time in high school or junior high at a swimming party. The girls were perched on the shoulders of the boys like riders astride of horses, and the game was to see which rider could throw another off her mount into the water. He had loved the game. In the midst of it he had noticed his mother at the side of the pool, waiting to give him and his friends a lift home in the car. As soon as he and she reached the privacy of his house, she had told him not to play that game again. "A girl should not put that part of her anatomy," she had primly explained, "in touch with a boy's body." He remembered his astonishment at hearing this sentence and how, as she spoke, he could still feel the touch of the girl's thighs on his neck and shoulders. He could not remember how, if at all, he had answered his mother at the time. He knew that inwardly he had rejected her advice, her thought. He knew also that he had been ashamed—partly shamed as she had intended and partly ashamed of her, of himself for being the son of a prude.

He remembered something else that he could not date in time, couldn't remember how old he was. It might even have happened more than once. She had told him it wasn't nice for girls or women to sit with their legs apart. Since most of the females he knew didn't often do that (it was before girls took to wearing slacks) this comment made no strong impression, until she went on to add that men should not sit that way

either. This had flabbergasted him, for to sit with legs together
or crossed meant that the masculine parts between the legs
were squeezed, which didn't seem right unless you were trying deliberately to get some sensation there. One sat with legs
apart in order that one's crotch could breathe. He didn't say
this. He only said, "Why?" She insisted that "spread eagle" was
not the posture of a gentleman. He was at the time—whenever it was—some years away from the declaration that he
was not a gentleman, which made her cry.

There was something wrong about opening your legs. This
was the message he accumulated, and while he had never for
an instant agreed with it in his mind, nor acquiesced with
his conscious will, he knew, had long known, that the message
had gotten through. To open his legs was an act of defiance.

He had no sense whatever of his father's legs. His father
was a short man, so he must have had short legs. He wore
white boxer underwear shorts: that was a clear memory. Of
his father's face, hands, skin, and smell he had the sharpest
of impressions. These had even grown stronger in the past
year, since his father died in old age. These tactile memories
were all warm and good. He had inherited his father's hands
and skin, as well as many of his mannerisms, and the recognition of this by himself and his friends and various relatives
gave him pleasure, although he had never consciously sought
to imitate his father. Only now for the first time did he think
to ask himself what memories he had of his father's legs, and
he drew an almost complete blank. Short, yes, as you could
notice in the trouser legs. He had often seen his father bounce
small children on his knee, and the theologian must have been
given such treatment as a child, but he could not remember.
He could recall his sister climbing onto their father's lap
when Daddy came home after work, and he remembered a
slight (was it slight at the time?) envy at the privilege of the
girl two years younger than himself. But there was nothing
here as strong as the negative valence about open legs he had
drawn from his mother.

He remembered also his sister's thighs. When he was eight or ten he had felt them with his hand. His objective at the time was to feel much more, but this was as far as she would let him go, and later she had told their mother on him, which led to a "talking to" the dialogue of which he couldn't recall. The scene of this anatomical exploration was as vivid in his mind as a movie, but its aftermath was not. He remembered the thrill of his forbidden moves, conducted in silence. And he remembered the excitement in his genitals. No doubt he had concluded from the episode that these things are the pathway to the region of No, but this was such an obvious conclusion it hardly needed to be reinforced by a memory as vivid as this. The scene was probably cathected by his love for his sister, which was another story.

This was the inventory he could make at the time. The lead that seemed "hot" was to his mother's shame or fear of the lower regions and to the psychic use which he had made of this in the economy of his growing up. He wanted now to walk a fine line. It was not to his purpose to blame any of his hang-ups on his mother. He had gone through that already, and in the course of recent therapy had vented quite a lot of hostility in her direction. The task now was to assess how he had played the cards life had dealt him, leaving off the childish complaint that the deck was stacked. But in this very task it was important to see what the cards were. Otherwise, the childish complaint would flip over to its equally childish opposite, the omnipotence fantasy that one dealt one's own cards and could do with them whatever one pleased, as if there were no limits, no finitude, no continuity in the structures of time. He was sure that the shame was there and that he had not, all on his own, invented it. Nor had his mother. She did not, he thought, make things up with which to torment him; these were her characteristic ways, the attitudes she had learned and formed in the course of her life. And he could see, as who couldn't, that genital shame went back a long way in the human race. You arrived, right soon, at the fig leaves of Adam and Eve. If original sin meant that there is a social, historical continuity to the barrier between the self and its instincts, a shame at being oneself, there could be no argument. Nor would you have to come then to the opinion of Rousseau that all is well in the state of nature and corrupted only by society. For you had merely to observe that society is man's natural state. Human beings are bio-cultural; child care, necessary to survival, socializes the child willy-nilly; and the notion of a human being in a state of nature and not in a society of any kind is a fantasy of abstraction.

So the sense of sin as transmitted from generation to generation was valid. What was not valid was to ontologize this, to read it as a curse or a Fall for which there is no remedy except divine intervention from outside of history, like Christ descending from heaven and somehow breaking the bond, and God at the end of time somehow redeeming us from having been born. The doctrine of original sin is, on its face and in its effect, anti-life; and this must not be allowed of any Christian doctrine, which is why the doctrine of celibacy, for instance, if it was ever any good, is not good now, and the same for the so-called "natural law" argument against birth control. You have in every case to get back to the life-affirmation that is the spring of Christianity, since the purpose of the gospel, as Jesus expressed it, is abundant life. It need not be added that "abundant" refers to quality as quantity, since the concept of life is itself qualitative.

He put his hand once more upon his leg.

They say that the divine antidote for sin is forgiveness. He thought this wrong, or a little beside the point. The real point, he believed, is love. What removes sin, or at least the power of sin, is not its being "forgiven" but the sinner's being loved. At any rate, he had not to "forgive" his thighs, much less imagine God would do so. What they wanted was attention, enjoyment, care, a certain honor—the opposites of shame, the attitudes of love. His hand resumed the caress. He opened his nerves to sense what the thigh, in truth, felt like. What does the hand find when it touches this flesh? What is there here of attraction and repulsion? He would invite to consciousness the suppressed sensations. No other way to love.

The discovery he then made was so simple it surprised him. That is, what surprised him was his previous failure to notice the obvious, to have been so out of touch with his own anatomy. He discovered the muscles in the back of his legs.

The muscles in the front of his thighs had never had any pain or given him any trouble. He liked them. They reminded him of his masculinity. It was those muscles he noticed in the legs of athletes as they tensed, for instance, in a jump on the basketball court. And those muscles were the ones he imagined when ancient warriors like Hector and Achilles boasted of their powerful thighs. The pronounced muscles in the front distinguished the male leg from the female, and while his own were not those of an athlete, he nevertheless took pride in them.

But at the back—or now, in the tub, on the underside—the thigh became soft, fleshy, feminine, obscure. Or did it? With time at his disposal, and in the resolve to find out the truth of the leg, he felt it first on the surface and then deeper. He probed and grasped with his fingers to see what was there. His touch passed through the fatty tissue and found, beneath, a bundle of muscle.

It surprised him to find muscle where none was expected, but the deeper surprise was the surprise itself. "Well, I'll be goddamned," he said.

He moved the right leg to see what these muscles were for. He hadn't the faintest notion. He was to find later, by interviewing his friends, that other people didn't know either. But it was fortunate that he did not yet know that his ignorance was shared, for that might have abated his curiosity. He found that the muscles in the rear of the thigh became very firm when he kicked down hard with his heel. He performed this exercise several times, and as he did so he was overtaken by a slowly gathering shock of recognition.

The force of his dawning awareness came from the con-
vergence now of several old pieces of knowledge he had not
previously been able to integrate or use. They all gathered at
once, and he had to separate them in order to think about
them. The first had to do with his frequent anger.

He had a strong temper and had been famous since childhood, in his family and among close friends, for occasional
outbursts of rage. In public he was not given to this; or rather
he "controlled" it, as his mother had told him he must, and it
came out, so he was told, in a very civilized demeanor that
nevertheless often communicated hostility and intimidation.
When he was angry *en famille,* his energy would rise to the
top of his body. His eyes became fierce, even wild; his voice
rapid, loud, and eloquent; his face flushed; neck rigid; fists
clenched and moving all over the place in gestures emanating
mainly from the elbows. His shoulders did not much get into
the act. If he was very angry, he would sometimes kick with
his feet in fast, short jabs. At the end of such an outburst he
was invariably reduced to tears.

This violent temper, which was frightening to behold and
which seemed to him so at odds with the character of a
teacher, theologian, and man of faith, had been the occasion
for much therapy in the past. It was less severe now than
formerly, whether because of the therapy, or because he was
mellowing in middle age, or both, he did not know. He had
learned from reading Rollo May that his anger was a *daemon,*
a part of himself that he tended to take no responsibility for
and that therefore turned against him. He was the principal
victim of his own rage. He knew that he was not in possession
of his anger precisely because he refused to possess it. The
more he treated it like an affliction, or a visitation of some
evil spirit, the worse it got. So he had for some time now
consciously affirmed this anger, regarding it as one of his own
attributes, and it had become less threatening and less frequent.

But he realized now that the change in his mental attitude,
very good as far as it went, was less than whole because it

had not included a transformation in the subjectivity of his body. It was, he thought, like a Christian conversion not consummated by baptism. It was hard in our culture to explain why a mental attitude needed a corresponding physical expression. The notion even smacked of irrationalism and brainwashing, of sympathetic magic and superstition. Most "respectable" discussion of it got bogged down, as far as he was concerned, in vain theories of something called symbolism. So, for instance, baptism became a so-called "symbolic act," which seemed to him a phrase of intellectual superstition, and people who talked this way seemed not to be in very close touch with the actuality of baptism as the subjective experience of immersion in water. Even Luther had talked of sacraments as "signs," and the famous ecclesiastical definition of sacrament is "outward and visible sign." But if my brother ducks me under water, that's not a sign but a deed, though the deed may spring from an intention and may carry a message. He thought that baptism was first of all a deed, something done and experienced, and that if it was also a sign or a symbol, that was a secondary, or at most a parallel, matter.

His anger, which was nothing if not a bodily response to some situation or other, whatever else it might also be—his anger, which was a deed done, or usually half done, could not be transformed at the mental level only. It wanted a full integration. He did not come to this conviction by theoretical deduction from premises, although he had been doing some reading along this line. What convinced him was the involuntary experience of anger when he flexed the muscles in the rear of his thigh. He was not conscious of any outer condition or person to make him angry now. On the contrary, the bath, the hour, and the solitude were most pleasing to him. Yet the extension of the leg and the thrusting of the heel, with his attention devoted to the behavior of the thigh muscles in this action, put him in immediate touch with an objectless anger. He felt it in the pit of his stomach. "God damn!" he said.

He flashed back to a mountain hike he had taken with

friends two years ago. It was the clearest former occasion he could recall of the rise in him of an anger he could find no excuse for blaming on anyone or anything but himself. Everyone was pleasant, the day fine, the mountain one he had long wanted to explore and not particularly difficult. Yet as he climbed he had become almost beside himself with anger. He had tried like the devil to find some slightest pretext in the company for venting his anger upon them, was quite aware of doing so, but they had given him no excuse, and he had had to realize that the anger was of his own making. It now came to him with a start that in climbing the mountain he would have made vigorous use of these muscles at the back of his thighs, though that would not have occurred to him then because he did not even know that he had such muscles. The anger was the discharge (however uneconomical) of an energy not focused on or integrated into the climb because the body and the mind were at war in the region of the thigh. Every exertion of that muscle group required an effort of blocking the awareness of it from consciousness. So, in addition to the energy needed for climbing, other energies were needed to carry on an internal war, to distract the self from identifying itself with the very muscles that were doing most of the work. The internal war was a closed system. Its fraction of his total energy could not flow outward. Frustrated, this closed-circuit energy looked for an outlet, like an electric current looking for ground. If only there was something out there to strike! Or better, to kick. The anger looked for an object, but he was too rational that day to find it, his friends too oblivious of his mood to cooperate. Needless to say, he reached the top of the mountain as exhausted as he was frustrated. His mood was then "dumpy" and "grumpy." They noticed that and decided wisely to pay no attention. He had not climbed a mountain since that day.

He began to think on his anger at home. It was clear to him that when he blew his stack at the wife or the kids he invoked everything at his command except the larger muscles. Of the very strong muscles in the body, he was conscious of using in anger only those of the jaw and the neck, which he clinched, although he actually bit somebody only once. These muscles are among the strongest in the body, but they are not the largest. The really large muscles are those of the shoulders, upper arms, diaphragm, back, and thighs. None of these was conspicuous in his anger, either to himself or to his adversary, as he had in fact been told without being able to make anything of the information. It was as if the anger was projected to the extremities of the body, evacuating the major centers of power and deep feeling. The tongue would let fly with words, the tongue of a serpent, rapid, volatile, wounding with venom. The eyes flashed fire. The jaw, loose and agile in talking, would in silence become a fortress. (Why, he wondered, does the word "fortress" have a feminine ending?) The arms flailed mostly from the elbows, the fists moving like big weights at the ends of sticks. The legs, if they got into the act at all, were used from the knees downward. Perhaps one knee would be drawn up as a weapon, and the foot might fly outward in a jab of sudden swiftness. The skin surface, all over, was highly charged with feeling. To touch it at such a time was to risk attack by an electric fan.

Frightful as all this was, it was also most curious. Had it ever been observed by a totally disinterested party, it would have appeared comic. It was as if he became as brittle as a marionette while pretending to the emotions of King Lear. You might be very afraid of what he would do next, but you could not be afraid of *him*, because in a curious way he was not there. "He's not all there," a bystander might have thought. And his wife thought that he was "beside himself," as the saying goes—which he was.

He knew all this from talking with her in the aftermath of such scenes. Had his anger been real—that is, fully convincing —one of two results might have been achieved. Either they would have split up, or the anger would have vented itself and not become chronic. She told him frankly that in spite of her fear when he grew irate she did not draw any conclusions because she did not know in the slightest what to make of his behavior. This, of course, made him fuss, to think that his performance was not taken seriously, especially as it left him, every time, quite exhausted. She told him, in her maddeningly feminine way, that it was a shame, since he spent so much energy on these scenes, that he did not enjoy them more.

Condescending as such a remark sounded to him (he would not, in this bathtub, speculate on *her* motives) it was exactly on the mark. Until now, he had not been able to see the aptness of it and had let it go as her way of being indulgent, motherly, and reproving all at once. Now it struck him that he did not, in fact, enjoy his anger; and for the first time he wondered if he was supposed to. The reason this occurred to him was his sudden awareness that he had never gotten his large muscles into the act, and this came to him because of the anger now associated with muscles he didn't even know he had. The *sine qua non* of enjoyment is the involvement of the whole self, the flow of sensation through the entire body. Block that and an experience may still be interesting, educational, or whatnot, but it will not yield enjoyment, let alone joy. If she said he did not enjoy his anger it was the same as saying he was not fully in it.

It was possible, of course, that he held back the involvement of his large muscles from his angry moments because he didn't want to hurt anybody. Was partial noninvolvement a way of restraining a lethal rage? Possibly. Or possibly that was the genesis of the pattern some time in infancy or childhood. But he thought of something more likely. He was not conscious of his mother's ever restraining him from killing anybody or even from hurting anybody physically, because he had not been given to such behavior. But he was very conscious of her attempts to restrain his feelings. For one reason or another, he had let her do it, in part at least. In this, society had been her ally, or she its agent, whichever. And another ally, the strongest of all, had been religion. When he thought of his religious upbringing, in spite of the fact that he was raised as a Southern Methodist, one of the more emotional brands of main-line Protestantism, he remembered it mostly as an inhibition of feeling. Methodism, as he had known it, was very good at training your attitudes, but it did so at the expense of your feelings. That is, it asked for the inculcated attitudes to be felt (he had heard plenty about John Wesley's heart-warming and about the testimony of inward conviction), but it did not encourage you to let spontaneous feelings influence your attitudes. And of all the spontaneous feelings it seemed to discourage, the chief was anger, even more than sex. Worse than a sexual prudery, Christianity came across to him, even today, as prudish about anger, hostility, and all the negative feelings.

It is hard enough to control one's own feelings, let alone somebody else's. There is only one way to do it, never wholly successful, praise God: to control feeling, you rigidify or deaden the body. He remembered those afternoon naps, obligatory when he was a preschool child. He could not be made to sleep, but he could be forced to remain still by threat of punishment for any sound of stirring. He wondered if his legs had ever been held down to prevent their thrashing about in anger, hunger, or something. He didn't know. He remembered a fight with his brother, unfinished because of maternal interference, when he had shouted, "I hate him, and he hates me!" To which she replied, "That's not true." It was not that remark that had inhibited his feelings, because he knew what he felt then and there better than she did. The restraint was her removing him physically from the fight, standing him in front of her chair till the feelings went down instead of out through his fists and legs. He remembered that when he was naughty to Johnny Huddle or to old Mrs. Snotnose who lived down the street, he had to get dressed up in nice clothes and go with his mother to stand at their front door and mumble some sort of apology, his body hardly daring even to tremble with the rage he was afraid to let himself feel. Hold the breath.

Make small motions only. Be a nice little man (translation: a stick on a string). Control your temper.

Maybe it was good for him, who knows? Nevertheless, it would have to be undone.

"And how is the good boy today?" John Pierrakos was talking, but the tone (if not the exact words) was that of the "good boy's" mother, whom John could imitate without ever having met. The question paralyzed. The puppet answered, he couldn't remember what.

Pierrakos was his therapist, a year or so before the bathtub. The therapy had included much direct work with the body. The only thing the couch had been used for was kicking, pounding, and screaming.

How the business about the thigh muscles had been missed at that time he couldn't imagine, but matters quite close to it had been noticed, and he remembered them now. For instance, Pierrakos had noticed that he had an obstruction or block in the thighs. He would observe the theologian's posture and the way his body behaved in motion. One day he had put his fingers around the thigh and said, "It's as if there were a tourniquet here." The theologian had not replied to that. He remembered thinking, Is that so? So what? He hated the instruction to lie down on the couch and kick, but he always obeyed it like a good boy. Pierrakos clearly hoped that he would one day get angry during their hour and throw off the good boy behavior, but he had never done so by kicking. The only time he was truly angry with Pierrakos was when the therapist kept him waiting forty-five minutes for his appointment. Seeing this anger, Pierrakos handed him a baseball bat made of foam rubber, and he had flailed the tardy therapist with it with all his might. That felt so good he thought it worth the price of admission to all the months of therapy. But he had never, not even then, gotten in touch with the anger in his legs. So it was not quite true to say that he had swung the bat with all his might. "Whatsoever your hand finds to do . . ." He remembered the quotation. And he remembered

Kierkegaard's line: "Purity of heart is to will one thing." Gemini had never had a pure heart. Was that why he had chosen to be a theologian and an actor and a drama critic? He had pretty much given up the critic's role. But he believed that the task of the theologian, like that of the actor, was to go beyond the split, to find, in a lifetime of work, the purity of heart beneath the mask.

Pierrakos also noticed the theologian's feet, and what he said about them had wounded the patient's narcissism as deeply as anything ever had. He said that the arches were too high.

Now, the theologian prided himself for being light on his feet. Furthermore, he thought that the high arch of his foot was graceful. It more than made up for any inferiority he might feel when people, especially shoe salesmen, noticed that his feet were small. Big men have big feet, and he certainly wanted to be a big man. But he scorned flat-footed people, as he scorned flat-footed statements. He was proud of his arched foot, of the arched comments he could make, and of his whole sense of being able to maneuver like Hermes. His fantasy, which he'd never told anyone, was that he was a messenger from the gods. It was the redeeming side of his being a theologian, otherwise a ponderous calling. He detested reading most theologians because their style was flat.

And Pierrakos said his arches were too high. Couldn't the poor fellow notice their grace?

Still, he had enough grace to ask why, and promptly found out. For Pierrakos noticed not simply the feet but also their relation to the whole body. He noticed the size of the body frame, the height of five-eleven or so, and the weight of some one hundred seventy pounds; and he said that the acute arch of the foot on a body of such a size suggested that the weight was not being given fully to the ground.

It belonged to the therapy they were doing to stress the grounding of the body and the psyche. The theologian liked this metaphor. It made all kinds of sense.

But the theologian was a sky person. He was Hermes at heart. He had arched and tender feet, and for him grounding was not easy. There was even lurking in him the aviator's negative sense of the phrase, "to be grounded."

Had it not been for the anger, for those flights of rage, so clearly dysfunctional, maybe sinful, in his life, he would not have taken the notion of "grounding" so seriously. He simply could not escape the truth of it when Pierrakos spoke to him in the following way, saying, "You fight like someone not sure of his ground."

Jesus! Did he ever! The rage—he knew it instantly—was a cover for insecurity. In fact, he never expressed the rage except in a situation so secure that when the seizure passed he could lapse into impotence. More. In a public argument he had two techniques, invariably using one or both of them no matter how convincing the substance of his argument might otherwise be. One was to fire out a whole string of ideas so fast that his opponent could hardly keep up with them. This gave him the reputation of being "brilliant," and people who complimented him on this quality to his face refrained from adding what a few intimates sometimes went on to say— namely, that the brilliance also dazzled and therefore confused even his supporters. Yet even when he heard this, he attributed his behavior to the cunning of Hermes.

His other technique, more of a giveaway, was to plead. For instance, he had a long record of not being able to persuade committees to go along with his proposals. So he took to begging them to see his point of view. Sometimes he would literally implore. But mostly the plea was communicated by tone of voice. Looking back on his hundreds of sermons, lectures, and written pages, he realized that their tone was more hortatory than declarative. He was not inclined just to state something and let it stand on its own weight. He would justify it, explain it, repeat it, in the secret hope it could not be refused, and the still more secret fear that it might be. He did not like to listen to his own voice on tape. That's a common reaction to a tape or a photo of oneself, but he enjoyed his own pictures while cringing at his own voice. When he asked himself why, he realized it was because of a certain whining inflection, some lack of resonance, a perhaps not too covert plea to the listener to listen to what he said. It was the tone of a person convinced of his message yet not sure of his ground. Pierrakos also noticed this.

He had learned somewhere along the way that voice production begins in the region of the pubic bone. But such was his hermetic isolation from the ground that knowledge of the pubic origin of the voice had not caused him to think downward. Instead, he thought only of the voice rising through the body cavity, over the vocal cords, out the mouth and into the air. He did not even ponder the physical principle that an energy moving in one direction requires an equal and opposite force in the other. The farthest down he had ever thought about voice was when he had discovered, maybe three years before, that to hit and sustain a high note while singing hymns in church, it helped if he relaxed his anus. He felt a bit dirty to have made this discovery in church. But church was the only place he ever sang much, and he rationalized the matter by thinking that if it made the hymns sound better to the ears of almighty God, then it was justified. But he was troubled by his lingering childhood impression that people in church had no business having anuses, much less allowing them to open. What if this became public knowledge? What if the minister should invite the congregation to open their anuses and sing? He comforted himself with remembrance of Martin Luther's scatological mind, and wondered what Luther thought about in church.

The theologian and the therapist worked many months on grounding. It was good work, and he probably would not have begun, certainly not finished, the bathtub ceremony without it. But the therapy had not, while it was going on, uncovered the missing link, which was the obliviated muscles in the rear of the thighs of both legs. He was sure of it now.

More than like a tourniquet, it had been like something missing; and his task now was to reclaim it. Until this link was forged, he would have only half of his true connection with the ground. Whatever deprived him of that would limit his energy, stability, and power.

He flexed his legs again, one at a time. As he did so—this was hard to explain—he allowed himself to go with them. To tauten the rear thigh muscles, he pushed his heels out. It would have been usual for him, in making such a gesture, to push the heels *away* from himself, as if they were some kind of missile sent out beyond the statutory limit of his persona. Now he consciously made the identification. "*I* stiffen, *I* extend, *I* push against the tub." He went down into his legs and heels.

The result was a further surprise. In the aftermath of this movement a flood of feeling rolled upward in his body. It started in the heels as they touched the hard, cold porcelain of the tub. Then it traveled up his legs as a warmth of sensation. It flooded the whole of his thighs and from there spread into his groin and lower abdomen. The whole region was alive with feeling, and so excited was he by this vibrancy that his whole back tingled and shivered. He tilted his head backward and opened his mouth wide, pushing hard with his heel and feeling the muscles of his face stretched in a wide, open-mouthed grin. He exhaled strongly and relaxed into the water. He could not remember a time when he was more at one with himself.

For the first time in more than an hour he put weight on his legs. He drew them under him and got first onto his knees. He rocked like this for a few moments. Then he moved his foot under him and squatted, letting his tail dip in the water. He felt the weight of his torso on his thighs, and the weight of all on his feet, his ankles stretched and supple in the balance. Then he began to stand. He came up slowly. It was important to follow the burden of his weight as it was lifted by those muscles in the thighs. He realized with a start that these were the muscles needed to get him to an upright position. The symbolism of that was staggering. He was a man, quite literally, who had not known how he lifted himself. He resisted following out the symbolism. That was for later. It was more important to notice the muscles doing their job. He felt them contract, wishing he knew more about the mechanics of their attachment and the reciprocal arrangement of those in front and those in back. But he went with what knowledge he had. He felt the weight push down and the muscles pull, so that the bone took the weight, and the firmness came into the back of his thighs and then the calves, and he felt the push of his feet against the bottom of the tub. Then he was nearly straight up, and he pushed through his thighs to his heels, and his head was erect and he was looking out the window at the strong light of the day on distant hills.

He lifted his left leg and stepped out onto the floor. Then he lifted the other leg and reached for a towel. The linoleum of the floor was cool and soft. He dried first his thighs, massaging the backs of them and feeling the muscle under the fat. His legs felt different. While there was plenty of fat and he had to stand with feet wide apart to dry the inner softness, still each thigh had more muscle than he had supposed. As he bent and rubbed, he could feel it working to maintain his balance and to give mobility to his back.

He finished drying and went into the bedroom. The whole house seemed still to be asleep, and his wife had not stirred. He put on his clothes and went downstairs. At the kitchen door, as he opened it, he was met by the gigantic Labrador pup, agitated from head to tail, avid for company, excitement, and the freedom of the out-of-doors. It did not bark, but it scampered and breathed so loud that he shshed it so as not to rouse the sleepers. He put on some water for coffee and went with the dog outside.

He could not tell if he was more fascinated by the earth beneath his feet or by the radiance of the morning light. The dog ran in the manner of random spirit such animals display when they know not which attraction to follow. He watched it lift its thigh to piss at least a score of times.

He was drawn to the flower garden. It was carefully but not primly cultivated. It was a square rimmed by a low stone wall. The center was grass, and the beds occupied the four sides. Everything was lush green, and the peonies, marigolds, and a few other June bloomers were speaking in color. There were tiny droplets of dew. He stood in the middle and looked at each flower and leaf.

Praise is not quite the word for what he felt. That word obscures the keen perception of his sight. Communion is a better word, though still too pious. He was conscious of a deep transaction between himself and the place where he stood. He and the flowers both sent down roots. He was not sure but that his were deeper than theirs. Still, he had no desire to make invidious comparisons. This thought put him on to what he meant. We send down the roots that we need. The earth receives our search for an adequate grounding.

He had not, until today, put down deep roots. Figuratively, yes. But the body is not a figure, though it may cut one, and the self is not a type. We put down the roots that we need. In the maturity of his life the symbols had proved too shallow. He wanted to go deeper. He wanted the firmer soil of the literal truth. Symbols, he knew, grew from the deep. If not, they withered. The God he believed in was not a symbol. He was the deep from which the symbols grew. Last night his friend had said: "There are earth mothers and sky fathers. We need some earth fathers."

His foot pressed the soil. His thigh pushed it there. He inhaled. He turned toward the house, the dog frolicking after him. The other dog barked inside the house. His friends would be up. He walked on his earth father/mother toward the house. The symbols fell away. Neither father nor mother would emblem what he felt. He was full of an energy that has no name.

VI

BODILY THEOLOGY

John Y. Fenton

> Escape from the body is escape from being man and escape
> from the spirit as well. Body is the existence-form of spirit,
> as spirit is the existence-form of body. (DIETRICH BONHOEF-
> FER, *Creation and Fall*)

Christian theological concern with the human body has been
a complex mixture of Old Testament and Hellenistic strains.
Although it proclaimed a strong message of the sanctifiability
of the body, especially in its incarnational emphasis, Christian
theology nevertheless predominantly relegated the carnal
body, the flesh (*sarx*), to the domain of "this world" while
depicting Christian faith as primarily "spiritual," as not of
this world, and certainly not as carnal. (The resurrection body
is transformed, not flesh.) Genuine faith was depicted as primarily of transcendent origin stemming, on the one hand,
from the divinely implanted or bequested drive toward God
in the creature (especially in the Augustinian tradition) and,
on the other hand, from the transcendent God "in whom we
live, and move, and have our being." In either case, the
true life of faith is not something that springs from our
creatureliness, or our contingency, or our bodies, except
insofar as these may—whether by reflection, by analogy,
by participation, or by imaging God—somehow be made

acceptable ingredients to take part in the loving of God.

As I reflect upon some of the questions involved in bodily theology, and as I do this with the discussions of the Conference on Theology and Body now in the past, one basic issue stands out prominently for me: Is the possible positive significance of our bodies in theologizing based upon the simple carnality of our creaturely bodies or is this significance based upon the participation of our bodies (as well as our heads—and spirits, whatever they are) in something transcendent to them without which bodily participation in theologizing would not be justified? Are our bodies acceptable only because the notion of spirit or Spirit can be expanded to include our bodies? More simply stated: can we do bodily theology and can we do it simply as bodies? At least in the context of this book, additional theological examination of the rationale for a bodily theology seems necessary as well as some indication of the nature of the task involved in putting a bodily theology together.

I have been reluctant to accept the label or to label myself as a theologian in the past, preferring to think of myself as doing philosophy of religion with a primary interest in the history of religions, especially Hinduism and Buddhism. But the appropriate task for me in this essay appears to be essentially theological in character. For I must deal not only with the question of what the expressions of the Christian faith have been in the past, but also with what I believe the import of my Christian faith to be about my and your human body, and the place of our bodies in the world and in relation to God. It is because of this admittedly theological interest and because of my awareness as a historian of religion of the recent popularity of "Asian mysticism" in the United States, that I feel it necessary to deal with this question. For, in arguing that bodily theology is healthy Christian theology, I cannot avoid the question of what this body is and what, as I am able to understand it, the specifically Christian appreciation of the body and its relation to God is.

To far too great a degree in the past, Christian theology's concern with the body has been confined to what theology has to say about the body, it being assumed that theology comes from outside the body, and that theology approaches this flesh as something it will try to interpret from its superior vantage point. In more recent times of course, the growth of the physical and social sciences has provided vast amounts of new information and theories about human beings as biological, psychological, and social organisms. By and large these studies are carried out without reference to theology, following the renaissance dictum that the proper study of humans is the human species itself. Unfortunately, theology has far too often returned the compliment by taking the general point of view that the subject matter of Christian faith —whatever it is—is not the same thing that the social and biological sciences are studying. Various scientific theories have a degree of influence on theologizing, but these theories are carefully insulated from the supposed heart of the theological concern, which is something properly and specifically religious or faithful. The theological concern is with the Ultimate, the Sacred, the Supernatural, or Being-Itself; the sciences deal with the preliminary, the profane, the natural, and the relationships between beings. In general then, although there are some notable exceptions, theology has not come to grips with the sciences as constituent rather than merely auxiliary to the theological process. The objective scientific study of the behavior of the human body is not, however, the same as the attempt to comprehend the body as a participatory experience. To expect that theologians who consider the behavioral study of the body as not really theologically relevant should open themselves to the constitutive character of their own body experience is perhaps the height of optimism. This is nevertheless what I am suggesting and what I hope will begin to bring a positive theological response. It is time for theologians to raise the question: What has the body to tell us about theology?

Bodily theology is not merely a theological description of the body, a set of admonitions or rules about the proper use of the body, or an understanding of the body as an expression of, or housing for, the spirit or soul. Rather, for a bodily theology, it is the body that is *donum*. It is the body that is given to us to experience, given for us to experience, and given as our experience. Soul, spirit, God, and theology are the questions, not the starting points. For a bodily theology soul, spirit, God, and theology must be understood as functions of our bodies, not the other way around. To make this affirmation is, as I understand it, not to be anti-Christian at all. It is to reexpress the ancient Christian heritage, especially its Old Testament and Jewish tradition as we can understand it in our present time, and to take up a non-Cartesian alternative for the understanding of human creatures.

The message that gets across to members of non-Christian cultures when what Westerners take to be Christian spiritualism is transmitted to them is sometimes surprisingly different from what was intended. Maurice Leenhardt, missionary to the Canakas of New Caledonia, tells of a conversation he had with a convert to Christianity toward the end of his forty-five-year mission. Leenhardt was keenly interested in the world view of the Canakas and the ways in which it changed through Christian and French influence. He suggested to the native convert that the new element that the Christian message brought to the Canaka was the notion of spirit. The native replied that this was not the case at all. The Canaka already had a notion of spirit. What Christianity brought was the conception of body. Before Christianity came, the Canakas had no notion of themselves as distinct persons. The new notion enabled them to grasp the notion of space, and thence distance, separation, and personhood.[1] (Is the Christian message primarily a revelation of the body rather than the spirit?)

This initially surprising response of the Canaka points to a distinctive element in the Christian doctrine of the body that becomes even more clearly delineated by comparison with

some predominant Hindu and Buddhist attitudes toward the
body. A brief description of these attitudes may set the implications of non-bodily theologies in bold relief. Yoga and
Advaita Vedanta share a typical Hindu attitude. For both
traditions the problem of the human condition is the individual's confusion of the self with the non-self. The non-self
in question is primarily the individual's body. The body is,
for both traditions, a limitation to be overcome.

For the Yoga of Patanjali it is thought possible to overcome
our bodies because our true self is non-bodily spirit. Patanjali's
concise definition of the aim of yoga is *chitta vriddhi nirodha*
(cessation of consciousness of and reaction to any stimuli external or internal to the physical body). This indicates that
the body and its drives must be put under total control and
finally be rendered inert so that the eternal, divine, and infinite spirit (*purusha*) of each of us may enjoy its own om-
niscience, necessary reality, and boundless bliss without any
further interference from the physical body. The body is at
most the context in which the struggle for the release of our
divinity is to be carried out. It is our fundamental, individual,
and plural divinity that makes it possible to cut off all dependence of our spirit from our body. Yoga is concerned with
the body only to the extent necessary to overcome it. "I am
spirit (a god). I am not my body."

Classical Yoga is frankly dualistic, believing that both
matter and spirit are real but that the dependence upon matter can be broken. Advaita (non-dual) Vedanta maintains
that both the body and the apparent plurality of selves or
spirits have only a practical reality. Ultimately reality is non-
dual and this non-dual reality is the true Self of my self and
of all things. Advaita Vedanta shares with Yoga the view that
the body is basically limiting and that limitation as such is
to be avoided. The body is born, decays, and dies, but our
true desire is to be unborn, to overcome fragmented existence
in a plane of reality that is always real, true, and blissful without limit. Simply to free our spirits from our bodies (as in

Yoga) would be to be still limited in the Advaita Vedanta view. Our spirits would still be separate, and still—although no longer bodily—fragmented. Diversity as such is a limitation for non-dualism, so it is proclaimed that ultimate reality is not diversified at all.

In both of these Hindu traditions the body is given short shrift. The body is something to be mastered, then left upon a lower plane of concern, and finally to be of no concern at all. Finitude as such is evil and the body is finite. Both traditions are based upon the belief not only that the human being has an innate desire for the Infinite, but also that this desire in the human being is satiated only by his becoming Infinite. Satiation is possible because we are already Infinite. We have only to realize our essential Godhead to overcome our bodies and the world.

In one of the more popular (but less well known in America) Hindu traditions, Visistadvaita (non-dualism of diversity), the problem of the human body is understood in ways more generally like those of Western Christianity. The body is taken much more seriously than in Yoga and Advaita since it is regarded not only as real, but also as in some sense constitutive of the human being as long as he lives. A central model for this tradition is that the world is the Body of Brahman. All that exists is contained in God as his Body. This Body of God consists of conscious selves or souls, and unconscious matter (including the physical body). Souls (*jivas*) are real and plural; matter is real and diversified; and this is somehow the case without threatening the basic non-duality of Brahman. One might expect the role of the human body in the theological process and in the process of salvation to be much greater in this tradition and to some extent this is the case (there is much heavier emphasis upon morality and religious duty). But, in a way reminiscent of many Christian theologies, the world is seen to be hierarchically organized with matter, including the body, the least valuable constituent of the world process. Our selves are "fallen" when we are ruled by our bodies, when we obey the most natural tendencies of our biological organisms. The body should instead be ruled by the self, but this is possible only if the self is ruled by God, who is our innermost Self. Thus determined by the Inner and Outer Transcendent God, the self is freed from dependence upon its body, becomes dependent upon God instead, and then spiritually dominates and redirects the functions of its body. Radhakrishnan states:

> The problem facing man is the integration of his personality, the development of a divine existence in which the spiritual principle has the mastery over all the powers of soul and body.[2]

Finally, it should be noted that, as in Yoga doctrine, the human body has no function for the released soul after death. It falls away, and the soul alone communes with God in heaven, becoming like him in every quality except the capacity to create and destroy the world. Again the soul is seen to be essentially omniscient, infinite, eternal, and able to satisfy all of its desires. It can rule its body and, eventually, leaving it behind, can recover its essential non-carnal nature.

All three of these Hindu traditions are articulated dualistically. The self or Self is spirit with all or most of the qualities of divinity. The body is either neutralizable, non-real, or completely dominable by spirit. The spirit is free and immortal; the flesh is bound, mortal, and corrupted. What is wrong with this orientation? For me an answer can only be given in normative Christian terms. Non-bodily theologies are anti-self, anti-neighbor, anti-society, and anti-world. Only part of me is acceptable, and then, not because it is me but because it validates me from beyond myself. If I am acceptable at all, it is not due to my particularity, but to my transworldly divinity. My neighbor is also of only transcendent interest. If I love him, it must be only for the sake of the Spirit (Self) within him. Nothing else is really valuable. Confronting my neighbor should be simply another occasion to see God. Society and world are valuable only as arenas in which individual liberation may be achieved; they have no intrinsic value as part of the created order of things.

There are, of course, other Hindu traditions with greater emphasis upon the role of the body and with stronger emphasis upon the materiality of the world, and all Hindu religious theories must be balanced against the facts of Hindu society and history. It is our purpose here, not to review the whole Hindu tradition, but to point to the logic involved in non-bodily theologies. Something similar is at work in non-bodily Christian theologies.

Theravada Buddhism's attitude toward the body is in many respects highly suggestive. The idea of soul or spirit is given up. What I call my "self" is really a temporary, dynamic, bodily continuity. There is no immortal soul and no God to which to retreat from the corruption of the body. But all pain is mental, something added to experience. The trained and transformed consciousness can receive everything as it is in tranquillity. I am not my body and there is no real I. While this point of view may appear realistic, this judgment is questionable from a Christian standpoint. The bodily functions become just as sublimated and subdued in the Theravada Buddhist path as in the Hindu traditions we have discussed. One is trained to treat the body as a loathsome, foul-smelling thing. Basic bodily drives are to be overcome and tranquilized by rigorous restraints, and objective observation is focused so as to neutralize any delight, passion, or fear. The joy of life is in regarding all things the same, in imperturbability and peacefulness. Theoretically, of course, if all things were really regarded as the same in Theravada Buddhism, the normal drives of the human body, including sexual needs, should be as welcome as any others. (This implication is developed in other forms of Buddhism, especially Tantra.) But the body is basically suspect. It is a snare that continually conditions us to seek pleasure and to avoid pain, and it is the basic source of the false notion that we are egos who must defend themselves. Therefore the body must be subdued, its messages to consciousness stilled by being systematically observed in detachment.

Thus Theravada Buddhism offers merely a new method and rationale for overcoming the body, not a new openness to the positive function of the body in full human life and therefore in full spiritual life. The body is a problem to be overcome in these traditions. Liberation is from the body, and from the ego: it is "overcoming the human condition." [3]

Basically the Christian objection to all these doctrines is not that they are psychologically or physiologically useless—there is a great deal that we can learn from these traditions. The objections to these doctrines are rather that they run counter to the Christian positive valuation of the whole human being as creature of God, that part of the creation is treated as something to be escaped or rendered completely inert or mechanical, that so little value is attributed to the particular finite perfections of individuals as individuals, and finally that all true value is or is completely derived from a plane of "reality" that shares nothing in common with the human condition. The "unborn" is the ideal, not the alive.

A case can be made that non-bodily Christian theology has many of the same fears and motives as the Hindu and Buddhist theologies. What is behind the Christian doctrine of the immortality of the soul? Is it not, like the Hindu doctrines, motivated by a desire to escape the corruptibility of the body? In contrast to the resurrection doctrine that we are living bodies, is it not an attempt to overcome the human condition? Are we not desiring to be eternal like God, in at least this respect to be divine ourselves? Is not the claim that the essence of the soul cannot die a claim to divinity?

Objections to non-bodily theologies could, of course, be raised on psychological grounds, and this has been done to a considerable extent during the Conference on Theology and Body. I will discuss the issues primarily on theological grounds. As I understand it, the Christian tradition fundamentally affirms a strange and perhaps unique doctrine: the creation is good and acceptable even though it is finite, even though it is merely creation, even though it is not divine, even though its worth does not depend upon its being in some way part of God's nature or of his body. That the creation can be both non-divine and good at the same time—and that the whole of creation is good and non-divine—is a symbol complex which it has been very difficult to hold together in Christian theology, especially under the influence of Greek philosophy. The elements-in-tension in this complex have too often been felt to be incompatible. Finitude, contingency, imperfection when compared with absolute imperfection, and the necessity of death—these have too often been felt to be unbearable. So either the creation must somehow participate in the Creator and share his infinite and perfect nature; or finite creation becomes acceptable only when it is in some way supernaturalized by God and divested of its original qualities; or only the infinite God is good and everything else called good is so only by derivation or (often temporary) donation; or only part of the creation is good (the divine part) such as the soul, the religious feeling, the depths of the unconscious, the moral sense, Objective Reason; while the rest is not good. The tension between Creator and creation is difficult to understand, much less to live with. But in this tension is what I believe to be one of the most distinctive contributions of Christian tradition to the history of the religiousness of the human species. The very incompleteness of this idea is part of its peculiar flavor, for it is the incompleteness, the interdependency of things that we are here made free to love and celebrate. Even the freedom is strange because it too is dependent and conditioned; but this is the human condition and it is proclaimed good! We may love ourselves and love others for their own sakes, even though neither we nor they are divine.

Once we can affirm the goodness of our creatureliness, we no longer need the idolatry of the immortal soul, or the immortal mind, or the immortal archetypes, or of Objective

Reason. Both the doctrine of rebirth and the doctrine of the immortal soul are repressive. If we could lose our desire to be something other than what we are, then the way could open to appreciate what we are as human beings, as creatures of God; then the need to divide off the creation into divine and demonic parts would also begin to erode.

The creation is good and non-divine and the *whole* of creation is good and non-divine. If the creation is neither divine nor demonic, but good in its basic creatureliness, then the arbitrariness of non-bodily theology should become apparent. This may be illustrated in psychological terms. Our earlier quotation from Radhakrishnan indicates how closely dominance over the body by spirit is tied to the ideal of psychic or personal integration. Some part of an individual that is supposed to be more acceptable is focused, strengthened, and energized until it becomes dominant over the remaining unacceptable part of the organism. There are numerous ways in which part of the self can become dominant enough to provide this kind of basis for self-unification. Some of these can be seen clearly in mystical techniques such as the Theravada Buddhist practice of mindfulness or Advaita Vedanta meditation upon the Witness of experience. The trouble with techniques of this sort is not so much that they might not work or that they might have psychically harmful side effects or aftereffects. The trouble is rather that the bases from which they start and the methods they use are arbitrary, selective, and artificial in their rearrangement and transfiguration of things. Pieces of the self and of its environment get broken, crushed, devalued, and just plain left out and ignored as though they did not exist and had no right to be noticed. Again, the question is not whether this *can* be done, but rather whether or not it *ought* to be done. The Theravada Buddhist analysis of the self-protective selectivity of human apprehension, of the deliberately euphemistic rendering of experience by human consciousness, and of the amnesia and anesthesia of the anxious human ego not only describes the pervasive human techniques for making life livable, it also describes the basis for the success of most forms of meditation. Zen Buddhist meditation (*za-zen*) is more attractive in this respect since it does not appear to produce a unified personality, but rather a dynamic personal continuity of continual change in the present as circumstances change. But even Zen selectively cuts out memory of the past, anticipation of the future, and attachment to the finite and fleeting. As impressive as Zen is, one still wonders from a Christian perspective why the past must be repressed and the threat of the future not allowed to penetrate consciousness. Part of the creation is not good and must be suppressed, forgotten, arbitrarily not noticed. Otherwise, I will be vulnerable. I must forget that I exist, otherwise I will suffer. I am not I, but "no-self" and "No-Mind."

How then shall I "be not anxious"? Why am I anxious? Am I anxious because I am vulnerable? because I can be hurt? because I can be wrong? because I will die? Non-bodily theology seems to answer "yes." Unfortunately a great deal of the non-bodily theology in the Christian tradition finds the roots of anxiety in human contingency—in human liability to old age, sickness, death, impermanence, imperfection, and insubstantiality (like the Buddhists). In fact, the basic argument of such Christian theology is that it is human contingency that drives the human being toward that which is not contingent, namely, toward God. ("Our hearts are restless until they rest in thee.") While this more-or-less "ontological" approach to Christian theology may have its merits in other respects, on this issue it appears incoherently simultaneously to devaluate human beings at the same time that it divinizes them, resulting in a veiled but unmistakably dualistic conception of human nature. The human being is divided into "essence" and "existence" (Tillich) or "finite infinity" (Reinhold Niebuhr). Such conceptions recall the Hindu Shankara's characterization of empirical reality as "neither real nor unreal." To recover what the Christian message "be not anxious" might mean, I will propose an alternative appreciation of anxiety.

"Why am I anxious?" If the creation is good and non-divine, contingent, finite, imperfect, etc., then anxiety must have some other source than contingency and finitude. For if the creation is good, it is not the evil of creation that makes me anxious. Creation as such is not evil. This is a fundamental Christian view of existence. There is also a fundamental Christian association of anxiety with sinfulness.

In my understanding the central notion of sin in the Christian tradition is *aversio dei*, literally "aversion for God." I take this to mean not only that sin is "hate of God," but also that it is "competition with God," the attempt to deny God so that I may play God myself, so that I may establish my own divinity. At the end of the creation story in Genesis the "host of heaven" explain why Adam and Eve were driven from the garden: They wanted to be "like one of us"![4] Sinful man wants to be like God or to take his place. He wants to live forever, be remembered forever, have eternal meaningfulness, possess the Truth, conform the world to his model for it and of it, and to be invulnerable and impenetrably whole, dependent upon nothing but himself. Is it not already clear why sinfulness and anxiety are connected? Why am I anxious? Because I am contending with God. Because I cannot accept my creatureliness and therefore find it ominously threatening. Accepting my creatureliness means giving up my nostalgia for divinity and affirming my creatureliness as good, not merely "essentially" (whatever that means), but existentially as well. It is my inability to live out both the goodness and the non-divinity of the creation that is my anxiety. It is this inability that drives me away from the creation to God, that drives me from my body to my (surely) immortal soul, and that drives me from nature to my rational mind.

As long as we talk of the human being as spirit encased in a body, of "treasure in earthen vessels," we run the very great danger of trying to play God at the very moment when we pretend that we are most faithful. We play this game with our ideas of absolute truth and immortal souls, and with most of our ideas of revelation. But because God is God, we do not need to play God. It is enough to be bodies, to be finite, to be fragmentary, and to know God only in this way—in his mysterious affirmation of our acceptability as finite, bodily beings. God releases us from *aversio dei*, the attempt to find absolute excuses for ourselves.

There is nothing infinite about human beings. Even our dissatisfaction and our anxiety are satiable. Our drives are indefinite, changeable, and dynamic, but not infinite. If it is true that man's desire is really infinite, then he will not be satisfied with God either—*unless he can be God,* or be absorbed in him, etc. Rivalry and identification with God is what it amounts to, the pretentiousness of original sin. The desire to rest in God is just that: rest in God and joy in the good of the creation. We must recover our bodies and remember who we are. We are the temple of God, the body in which *he* is to be worshiped. "It is he that hath made us, and not we ourselves." It is he that has declared that we are good and has released us to worship him rather than ourselves. Holy release! What good news!

If the creation no longer need be divided into the divine and the demonic, into the incorruptible and the corruptible, less anxious understandings of human creatureliness become possible. Since it is no longer necessary to maintain that the human being is a soul who has a body, or a soul incarnated in a body, or a soul whose body is its expression, it is possible to entertain the notion that the human being *is* his body. My body is constitutive of my very creatureliness, not an accidental or temporary form that my creatureliness takes. I do not have to be something else in addition to my body to be good, to be acceptable, or to accept myself.

Exactly what this means in detail and how it may be possible to live out our lives bodily is not entirely clear. How I may live joyfully as a creature of God is a mission to which I am called, not a predetermined model for Christian existence or a universal "objective" answer to all of the perennial philosophical problems surrounding the self and the body. Nevertheless this conception of creatureliness does put the philosophical problems in a new context; soul and self need no longer be treated as identical notions. As Richard Zaner argued in his paper during this conference, it is difficult to collapse the self and the body into one complex without residue, for, while in some respects I am my body, in other respects "I" seem to be different or at least distinguishable from my body. The old Cartesian dualism is difficult to overcome. Perhaps, philosophically, the contextual or lattice logic that Zaner suggested will enable us to comprehend the body/self as a complex interdependent unity interdependently related to its environment. Or it may be that the "I" that seems to be different from its body can be adequately conceived as first one and then another part of the biological organism's feeling different or distanced from other parts. Perhaps the kind of polytheistic, non-integrated model of the person described by James Hillman will recommend itself to us.[5] Or it may be that we will not be completely able to dispense with dualistic conceptions of self/body. For a bodily theology these are secondary issues. All of these solutions become alternate possible models for understanding human creatureliness. The question of the self is no longer the question of the soul. Whatever model is used, it neither threatens nor supports human immortality or divinity. Whatever distinctions are drawn, whatever bifurcations may be difficult to overcome, they are all within the creaturely nature of the human being. These problems are within the human body/self complex, whether or not self can be completely understood in bodily terms.

It also becomes clear that the problem of how the self is related to its body *need not* parallel the problem of God's relation to the world. While, to be sure, self-body relations have provided and will continue to provide part of the metaphorical basis for talking about God, these must be used with great care lest we again fall into fantasizing that we are gods in relation to our bodies as God is transcendent to and imma- nent in his body, the world. The putative parallelism is, from the viewpoint of bodily theology, most delusive, and it feeds our contention with God. The conception of the self as bodily does not imply a bodily God. We do not have to worry about possible blasphemy in conceiving ourselves as mere bodily creatures.

Bodily theology is concerned with specific, limited human beings who are defined by their own particular condition in interaction with each other and with the realm of nature. Nature is not merely the home of human beings; but rather, as the creation of God, physical nature is constitutive of human nature and of human culture. The ecological crisis is already crumbling the easy assumption that nature is put here merely for the use of human beings and that nature is good only insofar as it is useful for ontologically superior human beings. For a bodily theology all of the creation is on the same ontological level, and each part of the creation con- tributes to the whole of the creative process. Among other things this entails a changed attitude toward the role of hu- man beings in the world and a willingness to begin to consider what is good for nature for its own sake, and not merely what is of instrumental value for human beings. It may also mean that human beings must discover means of communicating with nature reciprocally. For if nature is to be valued for its own sake, we will be able to discover that value only if we can somehow learn to receive it.

There is no universal human being and no universal person. Each of us can speak for ourselves in our particular condition and thus we must learn from our limitation to open up to the other limited and interdependent beings of our world. We speak from our bodies. We are specifically male or female; black, white, yellow, or red; young, middle-aged, or old; healthy or sick. We have particular bodily properties, ca- pacities, and limitations. We are our own histories in our specific space and time, and we can make judgments only from specifically where we are or can be. All of these conditions constitute the variegated, particularistic now, here, and who of the theological task, and these conditions constitute the basic need for comm-unity before theology can be properly done. No one of us can speak definitively for the whole. All must speak to each other and must learn to speak together. The old tension between order and anarchy must be replaced by a new alternative: comm-unity.

NOTES

1. Maurice Leenhardt, "Quelques éléments communs aux formes inférieures de la religion," *Histoire des religions*, ed. by Maurice Brillant and René Aigrain (Bloud & Gay, 1953), Vol. I, pp. 96–100.

2. Sarvepalli Radhakrishnan, *The Bhagavad Gita* (Harper & Row, Publishers, Inc., 1973), p. 45.

3. Mircea Eliade, *Yoga: Immortality and Freedom*, 2d ed., tr. by Willard R. Trask, Bollingen Series, LVI (Princeton University Press, 1970), pp. 34–35, 69 ff.

4. Gen. 3:22.

5. James Hillman, *The Myth of Analysis: Three Essays in Archetypal Psychology* (Northwestern University Press, 1972).

APPENDIX

BODIES/AN ARTWORK

Julia Fenton

It is impossible to escape this dialectic: to be aware that one is burning is to grow cold; to feel an intensity is to diminish it; it is necessary to be an intensity without realizing it. Such is the bitter law of man's activity. (GASTON BACHELARD, *The Psychoanalysis of Fire*)

Documentation

I. *Some notes:*

Art (from the base *ar-* to join, to fit together) work (from the base *werg-* to do, to act) artwork after the fact artifact (the fact of the fitting together having been done; the object of the joining action taken).

Body (the whole physical structure and substance of a man) being (where: some-where: somewhere) being (how: some-how: somehow) now.

Artifact art fact: object remainder reminder documentation.

Experiences are privately ultimate. (The artwork *Bodies* consisted of the experience at the artwork of each person who attended it.) (The artwork *Bodies* consists of the experiences of the artwork of each person who is aware of it at the moment of awareness.) Remembered experiences are subject to changing. (Past plans are plans past.)

Artifactually, the artwork *Bodies* is remindered in the documentation.

Experientially.

II. *Some artifacts (after the fact)*:

Prior to the artwork, one of two types of announcement was distributed to each regular conference participant and to some other persons. Equal numbers of these announcements had been printed; the announcements had then been intermixed (by using a random table of numbers). Thus, the decision as to what type of announcement each person received was determined by chance. One type of announcement stated, "You are invited to participate in a current artwork . . ."; the other stated, "You are not invited to participate in a current artwork. . . ." (See Exhibit A for full reproduction of each type of announcement.)

At the bottom of each announcement was a detachable 4" × 6" card that was identical for both types of announcement (with the exception of a one-letter code which distinguished the "invited" announcements from the "not invited" announcements). The card had a place for the person receiving it to print his/her name. There were instructions to check one of two alternatives: "I plan to attend" or "I do not plan to attend." Instructions were given to return this card to the artist.

The cards returned were sorted into four categories, according to the type of announcement and according to the response indicated on the card:
(1) Invited, plans to attend; (2) Invited, does not plan to attend; (3) Not invited, plans to attend; (4) Not invited, does not plan to attend. Within each category, the cards were ar-

ranged in alphabetical order by last name. Two identical tables were centered, facing the entranceway, in the room in which *Bodies* took place. Centered in a row on the table to the left were four $4'' \times 6'' \times 4''$ gray metal card file boxes. The boxes were labeled respectively, from left to right: (1) Invited, plans to attend; (2) Invited, does not plan to attend; (3) Not Invited, plans to attend; (4) Not invited, does not plan to attend. The alphabeticized cards for each category were placed in the appropriate boxes on this table.

Centered in a row on the table to the right were eight $4'' \times 6'' \times 4''$ gray metal card file boxes. The boxes were labeled respectively, from left to right: (1) Invited, plans to attend, attends; (2) Invited, plans to attend, does not attend; (3) Invited, does not plan to attend, attends; (4) Invited, does not plan to attend, does not attend; (5) Not invited, plans to attend, attends; (6) Not invited, plans to attend, does not attend; (7) Not invited, does not plan to attend, attends; (8) Not invited, does not plan to attend, does not attend.

Near the exit, a television camera was trained on the two tables in such a way that the picture was of the tables and their immediate surroundings. A small monitor, placed at the exit, was attached to the television camera and was positioned in such a way that one could watch what was happening in the room on the monitor but no one could see himself on the monitor at any time. The closed-circuit transmission was instantaneous; no videotape was made. No photography was allowed in the room during the period of the artwork *Bodies*. A station was set up in front of the entrance to the room in which *Bodies* occurred at which anyone (those who received announcements as well as anyone else) could indicate his intention to participate in the artwork by signing his name on a pad of paper. Each participant was then given an instruction sheet (a copy of which is reproduced as Exhibit B). Oral instructions given to participants were: "Sign your name on the pad provided; take the instruction sheet into the room and read it; when you have finished doing what you are going to do, leave by the exit." (The list of initials of persons signing to participate in the artwork is reproduced in Exhibit C. Since permission to publish their names was not secured from participants, initials instead of names are listed.)

The distribution of cards in the file boxes before the artwork began was as follows:

Invited, plans to attend

D.A., J.A., R.A., E.A., K.B., E.B., J.P.B., B.B., E.C.B., J.E.B., K.B., D.B., J.B.C., C.D.C., M.L.C., A.G.C., Mr. and/or Ms. B.W.C., and/or M.J.C., J.C., M.C., R.C., M.C., J.W.C., P.D., T.F.D., D.E., A.E., P.E., F.E., A.F., J.F., H.F., H.F., H.F., Rev. J.G., J.G., J.G., P.G., E.F.G., P.G., V.G., Q.L.H., C.H., K.R.H., A.H., T.H., L.H., C.H., R.H., A.I., R.J., N.K., M.J.K., K.L., G.L., J.L., E.L., S.M., E.M., M.M., A.M.-H., C.M., B.M., R.M., B.M., L.M., E.M., W.McF., S.McK., B.N., A.O., J.P., J.P., W.P., R.A.P., S.P., E.D.P., M.P., S.P., J.D.P., W.R., J.H.R., T.R., M.S., S.L.S., Ms. V.S., W.S., R.S., C.W.S., A.S., D.R.T., G.W.T., R.W.T., Ms. C.T., R.T., J.L.T., Jr., K.W., R.W., D.W., H.B.W., C.W., T.W., G.Y., D.Y., J.Z.

Invited, does not plan to attend

J.B., J.B., S.A.H., P.H., A.B.I., J.J., B.K., W.M., M.M., B.J.M., A.M., W.McC., J.R., L.S., L.S.

Not invited, plans to attend

L.A., W.A.B., M.M.B., S.F.B., R.B., M.J.B., N.M.B., D.C., G.P.C., M.B.C., J.E.C., K.C., M.C., D.D., M.M.D., B.D.D., M.F.D., C.E., M.E., M.L.E., C.E., J.F., J.F., K.F., P.F., B.S.F., D.E.F., M.G., S.G., D.G., P.H., W.B.H., A.H., D.H., M.H., J.G.H., Sr. F.I., C.W.J., R.K.J., F.D.K., S.K., G.K., C.K., R.K.,

D.S.K., B.H.K., H.K., L.G.K., M.A.L., C.L., M.B.L., T.L., J.L., Mrs. C.G.M., M.A.M., J.W.M., M.M., A.M., J.N., S.N., M.O'N., D.P., S.P., P.P., J.P., G.P., T.R., R.S., K.S., W.S., S.S., J.N.S., C.S., C.S., N.S., B.T., D.V., Mrs. F.W., C.W., B.W., J.C.W. III, D.R.W., R.W., J.W., J.W.

Not invited, does not plan to attend

D.B., A.B., R.C., Dr. W.R.C., N.C., S.C., D.E., J.E., G. G., A.H., B.H., E.H., J.H., R.H.L., D.M., J.McC., H.McL., A.McN., R.D.P., L.R., K.S., L.S., TeC.T.

Invited, plans to attend, attends
(No cards)

Invited, plans to attend, does not attend
(No cards)

Invited, does not plan to attend, attends
(No cards)

Invited, does not plan to attend, does not attend
(No cards)

Not invited, plans to attend, attends
(No cards)

Not invited, plans to attend, does not attend
(No cards)

Not invited, does not plan to attend, attends

(No cards)

Not invited, does not plan to attend, does not attend

(No cards)

The distribution of cards in the file boxes after the closing of the artwork was as follows (the order within each category below corresponds to the actual order of the cards at that time):

Invited, plans to attend

E.A., B.B., J.B.C., P.D., F.E., J.F., H.F., J.G., J.G., P.G., K.R.H., A.H., C.H., R.H., N.K., K.L., E.M., M.M., C.M., L.M., E.M., J.P., S.L.S., R.S., A.S., G.W.T., R.W.T., H.B.W., C.W., G.Y.

Invited, does not plan to attend

J.B., J.B., S.A.H., P.H., A.B.I., J.J., B.K., M.M., B.J.M., W.McC., J.R., L.S., L.S.

Not invited, plans to attend

L.A., D.C., M.B.C., D.D., M.M.D., C.E., D.E.F., S.G., D.G., P.H., W.B.H., M.H., J.G.H., R.K.J., H.K., T.L., J.L., Mrs. C.G.M., J.W.M., M.M., A.M., S.P., R.S., K.S., B.T., J.C.W. III, D.R.W., R.W.

Not invited, does not plan to attend

D.B., A.B., R.C., Dr. W.C., D.E., J.E., G.G., A.H., B.H., E.H., R.L., D.M., J.McC., H.McL., A.McN., L.R., K.S., TeC.T.

Invited, plans to attend, attends

J.A., D.A., R.A., K.B., J.P.B., E.C.B., J.E.B., E.B., A.G.C., M.C., R.C., C.D.C., M.C., J.C., M.C., J.W.C., T.F.D., M.F.D., P.E., C.E., A.E., A.F., H.F., Rev. J.G., P.G., E.F.G., V.G., C.H., Q.L.H., T.H., L.H., R.J.,[1] S.K., G.L., C.L., E.L., A.M.-H., S.M., M.A.M., B.M., R.M., B.M., S.McK., W.McF., G.N., B.N., A.O., E.D.P., S.P., S.P., M.P., J.D.P., W.K.P., R.A.P., W.J.R., J.H.R., T.R., M.S., Mrs. V.S., S.S., C.W.S., D.R.T., R.T., Ms. C.T., J.L.T., Jr., K.W., R.W., D.W., J.Z., D.Y.

Invited, plans to attend, does not attend

J.L.

Invited, does not plan to attend, attends

Mr. and/or Ms. B.W.C., or M.J.C., H.F., J.H., A.I., M.J.K., A.M., W.M., W.M., W.S.

Invited, does not plan to attend, does not attend

(No cards)

Not invited, plans to attend, attends

M.M.B., S.F.B., D.B., M.J.B., W.A.B., R.B., N.B., M.W.C., G.P.C., J.E.C., K.C., C.C. was here,[2] C.D.D., D.E., M.L.E., M.E., J.F., K.F., J.F., B.J.F., M.G., D.H., A.H., Sr. F.I, C.W.J., G.K., D.S.K., F.D.K., C.K., R.K., B.H.K., L.G.K., M.A.L., M.B.L., J.N., S.N., D.P., P.P., G.P., J.P., J.P., W.S., J.N.S., G.S., C.S., N.S., C.W., B.W., J.W., J.F.W.

Not invited, plans to attend, does not attend

P.F., M.O'N., T.R.

Not invited, does not plan to attend, attends

S.C., N.C., R.P., L.S.

Not invited, does not plan to attend, does not attend

(No cards)

Additional items found in the room at the closing of the artwork (and their approximate locations) were as follows:

(1) One red berry. (On the table to the right of the entrance.)

(2) The card of T.W. with an accompanying note which read, "Invited, planned to attend, forgot till too late, but attended anyway." (On the table to the right of the entrance.)

(3) The remains of a card that had been torn into several pieces. (On the floor near the television camera.)

Special thanks are extended by the artist to D. Ray Talley and William Ewing for their technical assistance and advice during this artwork.

NOTES

1. This card had purple stains and the remains of several purple berries on it.

2. This entry was handwritten on the back of an instruction sheet and filed in the place noted. The words written were followed by a small drawing of a "happy face."

EXHIBIT A

You are invited to participate
in a current artwork
by Julia Fenton

BODIES

Friday, October 5, 1973

at any time between
1:00—7:30 p.m.

Casual Reading Room
Law School Building
Emory University

NAME: _____
(Please print)

CHECK ONE:

I plan to attend ___
I do not plan to attend ___

PLEASE DETACH THIS FORM AND RETURN IT TO THE Y
REGISTRATION DESK

You are not invited to participate
in a current artwork
by Julia Fenton

BODIES

Friday, October 5, 1973

at any time between
1:00—7:30 p.m.

Casual Reading Room
Law School Building
Emory University

NAME: _____
(Please print)

CHECK ONE:

I plan to attend ___
I do not plan to attend ___

PLEASE DETACH THIS FORM AND RETURN IT TO THE N
REGISTRATION DESK

Exhibit B

BODIES

October 4 and 5, 1973

Instructions

On the table to the left, you will find file boxes marked:
1. Invited, plans to attend.
2. Invited, does not plan to attend.
3. Not invited, plans to attend.
4. Not invited, does not plan to attend.

On the table to the right, you will find file boxes marked:
1. Invited, plans to attend, attends.
2. Invited, plans to attend, does not attend.
3. Invited, does not plan to attend, attends.
4. Invited, does not plan to attend, does not attend.
5. Not invited, plans to attend, attends.
6. Not invited, plans to attend, does not attend.
7. Not invited, does not plan to attend, attends.
8. Not invited, does not plan to attend, does not attend.

In the file boxes on the table to the left are the cards filled out by the individuals who responded to an announcement concerning the artwork *Bodies*. Each individual's card is filed in the box appropriate both to the type of announcement received and to the response made by the individual at that time. Within each box, the cards are filed alphabetically by last name.

From the appropriate box on the table at the left, please remove the card with your name on it and move to the table to the right. At the table on the right, place your card in the box which corresponds both to the type of announcement you received and the decisions you made with reference to that announcement as it relates to your presence at this artwork.

Exhibit C

Persons who signed in at the entrance
   to the artwork Bodies

For convenience, two sign-in sheets were available at the entrance; these are presented below as *List 1* and *List 2*. The names on each list are in the order that the signatures were made. If a person wished to enter the room more than once, he or she was requested to sign in for each additional entry. The notation "—" is used below for those parts of signatures that were not legible enough for transcription.

List 1

A.H., P.G., M.C., M.C., R.M.Z., J.C., J.F., E.C.B., J.G., J.H.P. III, W.K.P., G.P., C.E., J.N., P.P., J.G., G.K., C.K., M.G., J.R., M.J.K., D.L.B., V.G., R.P.P., D.L.B., J.K.R., B.D.M., S.K., Q.L.H., V.S., G.—., C.M., —.M.F., J.H., B.E.T., Jr., K.F., E.E., K.F., J.H., B.N., N.N., J.W.—., R.B., H.F., B.F., M.A.L., J.K., B.C., J.E.—., H.W., K.C., R.R., D.M., B.C., A.J., C.S., D.Y., S.P., L.S., R.A., S.S., S.C., W.R., J.B., T.H., N.S., C.J., D.S.K., D.H., C.C., B.W., V.G., S.M., P.B., N.B., N.C., B.K., W.B., T.R., L.M., T.R., D.W., J.D., M.S., K.F., R.T., M.S., K.F., J.F., K.F., W.M., M.P., S.P., W.S., B.D., J.F., D.T., S.C., M.T., C.E., T.W., A.M.-H., J.N.H.

List 2

W.F.W., R.K.S., A.M., D.A., K.C., C.D., P.C., M.E., A.P., G.L., W.S., D.—.M., M.L., S.N., J.G., L.C., E.G., W.E.S., B.McF., M.C., D.C., J.P.A., J.C.W., L.H., P.F., M.S.D., J.L.,

A.E., S.W., J.—.R., C.A.T., M.W.C., F.D.K., R.J., B.E., B.D., —, R.K., T.F.D., D.H., J.C.Y., R.M., F.W., D.E., D.—., L.K.—., C.McG., D.McB., J.Z., J.W., J.W., T.G.C., J.S.—., D.B., E.B., M.E., E.D.V., Jr., R.W., C.W., J.L.T., Jr., B.W.C., M.J.C., A.G.C., J.W., D.T., B.E., A.W., R.G.T., M.M.B., M.T., H.—., S.B., C.S., J. and C.S., M.D.W., K.W.B., J.C., J.W.C., M.E., G.N., D.R.P., J.D.P., D.D.M., M.O'N., A.M., H.—., F.I., M.B., C.C.S., C.L., C.E., B.M., S.McK., K.B., C.E., H.—., E.—., P.E., A.O., A.I., E.L., N.S., P.L., R.T., M.S., J.J.N., L.K., G.—., C.H., G.M.

CONTRIBUTORS

BERNARD AARONSON is director of the Laboratory of Altered States of Consciousness of the Institute for Research in Hypnosis, Princeton, N.J.

WILLIAM A. BEARDSLEE is Professor of Religion at Emory University, Atlanta, Ga.

CECIL W. CONE is Dean of Turner Theological Seminary, of the Interdenominational Theological Center, Atlanta, Ga.

TOM F. DRIVER is Paul J. Tillich Professor of Theology and Culture at Union Theological Seminary, New York.

JOHN Y. FENTON is Associate Professor of Religion, Emory University, Atlanta, Ga.

JULIA FENTON is an artist of Atlanta, Ga.

JOHN W. GILL is pastor of the Metropolitan Community Church of Atlanta, Ga.

SAM KEEN is an "ex-theologian" and a free-lance lecturer and group leader and a Consulting Editor to *Psychology Today*.

GWEN KENNEDY NEVILLE is Assistant Professor of Sociology at Emory University, Atlanta, Ga.

RICHARD ZANER is Easterwood Professor of Philosophy at Southern Methodist University, Dallas, Tex.